CULTURAL
INTELLIGENCE

CULTURAL
INTELLIGENCE

People Skills for Global Business

DAVID C. THOMAS

KERR INKSON

BK

BERRETT-KOEHLER PUBLISHERS, INC.
San Francisco

Berrett-Koehler Publishers, Inc.
235 Montgomery Street, Suite 650
San Francisco, CA 94104-2916
Tel: (415) 288-0260 Fax: (415) 362-2512
www.bkconnection.com

ORDERING INFORMATION

QUANTITY SALES. Special discounts are available on quantity purchases by corporations, associations, and others. For details, contact the "Special Sales Department" at the Berrett-Koehler address above.
INDIVIDUAL SALES. Berrett-Koehler publications are available through most bookstores. They can also be ordered direct from Berrett-Koehler: Tel: (800) 929-2929; Fax: (802) 864-7626; www.bkconnection.com
ORDERS FOR COLLEGE TEXTBOOK/COURSE ADOPTION USE. Please contact Berrett-Koehler: Tel: (800) 929-2929; Fax: (802) 864-7626.
ORDERS BY U.S. TRADE BOOKSTORES AND WHOLESALERS. Please contact Publishers Group West, 1700 Fourth Street, Berkeley, CA 94710. Tel: (510) 528-1444; Fax: (510) 528-3444.

Berrett-Koehler and the BK logo are registered trademarks of Berrett-Koehler Publishers, Inc.

Printed in the United States of America

Berrett-Koehler books are printed on long-lasting acid-free paper. When it is available, we choose paper that has been manufactured by environmentally responsible processes. These may include using trees grown in sustainable forests, incorporating recycled paper, minimizing chlorine in bleaching, or recycling the energy produced at the paper mill.

Figure 2.2 on page 34 from *Handbook of Organizational Culture and Climate*, N. N. Ashkanasy, C. W. Wilderom, M. F. Peterson (Eds.) copyright © 2000 Ashkanasy, Wildcrom, & Peterson. Reprinted by permission of Sage Pulications, Inc.

Table on page 111 from *When Business East Meets Business West: The Guide to Practice and Protocol in the Pacific Rim*, by Christopher Engholm, copyright © 1991 Christopher Engholm. Reprinted by permission of John Wiley & Sons, Inc.

Library of Congress Cataloging-in-Publication Data

Thomas, David C., (David Clinton), 1947–
Cultural intelligence : people skills for global business /
    David C. Thomas & Kerr Inkson.
        p. cm.
Includes bibliographical references and index.
ISBN 1-57675-256-9
1. Business anthropology. 2. Management—Cross-cultural studies. 3. Corporate culture. 4. Intercultural communication. I. Inkson, Kerr. II. Title.
GN450.8.T47 2004
302.3'5—dc22

Copyeditor: Kate Warne; *Proofreader:* Mike Mollett; *Designer/Compositor:* Bea Hartman, BookMatters. This book was indexed by the authors.

09   08   07   06   05   04
10   9   8   7   6   4   5   4   3   2   1

Contents

Preface

As we were working on the final draft of this book in Vancouver, we were constantly reminded of the forces of globalization that are shaping the environment in which today's businesspeople must function. One day, taking a break from our writing, we took a walk on the seawall path that circumnavigates Stanley Park, an oasis of tranquillity in the busy city. We rarely heard the English language spoken by the scores of locals and visitors enjoying the sunny day; we recognized Cantonese, Mandarin, French, Russian, and a few more, but some languages and dialects were complete mysteries to us. The range of cultures we encountered in that short time may be slightly unusual, but only slightly, as migration patterns respond to rapid economic and political changes occurring around the world.

Developments in information technology have made barriers of time and space almost irrelevant. Most of the work on this book, for example, was accomplished by coauthors who live and work 12,000 kilometers from each other and who did most of the close collaboration at that distance, by e-mail.

What this globalization means for businesspeople is that the need to interact with people who are culturally different has never been greater and will only increase in the future. Cross-cultural people skills are important because managing people effectively is key to organizational effectiveness, and the people in organizations are increasingly multicultural. This book is about becoming more effective in dealing with people from different cultural backgrounds. It is about acquiring the global people skills that are important for twenty-first-century managers. It is for people who travel overseas and encounter new cultures, as well as for those who stay at home and find that other cultures come to them. It is about acquiring the *cultural intelligence* not only to survive without difficulty or embarrassment in the new global, multicultural business environment, but to pursue your goals in this environment with the confidence needed for success.

Although we encounter the multicultural world in many different areas of our lives—for example in social, educational, and leisure settings—this book is meant specifically for use in the multicultural business world. For this reason we call the readers of this book "managers." We are using the term "manager"—rather than the more accurate but also more cumbersome term "businessperson"—in the broadest possible sense. Here, a "manager" means anyone who is engaged in a business activity, including not just people with managerial responsibilities, but also people such as entrepreneurs, salespeople, office staff, and technicians—anyone who operates in a business setting and deals with others from different cultures.

This book is different from other books you may have seen about cross-cultural management or doing business in other countries.

First, this book is not country-specific. We do not provide laundry lists of drills and routines that should be applied in this country or that. Our intent is rather to help you to acquire a way of thinking and being that can be applied to any number of countries and cultures.

Second, this book is based on years of sound academic research. However, it is not an academic text, and we have tried to present important concepts in a straightforward way that will be appreciated by the busy managers for whom the book is intended. To make the learning concrete, each chapter is illustrated by a number of case studies in cross-cultural behavior, from various cultural settings.

Finally, we don't promise that this book will solve all your business problems. However, we sincerely believe that if you read and apply the concepts outlined here you will be well on your way to acquiring a critical core competence needed in business today—cultural intelligence.

Cultural intelligence is a new concept. However, it builds on earlier concepts that you have probably heard of: the intelligence quotient (IQ) and emotional intelligence (EQ), the idea that it is important how we handle our emotions. Cultural intelligence (CQ) incorporates the capability to interact effectively across cultures.

The concept is easy to understand, but it takes time and effort to develop high levels of cultural intelligence. If you are starting from a very low baseline, you may face years of studying, observing, reflecting, and experimenting before you develop truly skilled performance. However, becoming culturally intelligent is essentially learning by doing and has useful outcomes beyond the development of skilled intercultural performance. In addition, different cultures are fascinating, and learning them can be a lot of fun. This book is the place to start the journey.

Our first four chapters outline the fundamentals of cultural intelligence. Chapter 1 shows how a lack of cultural intelligence can negatively affect business interactions. It examines the problems with current methods of addressing these cross-cultural issues and identifies acquiring cultural intelligence as a more productive approach. The next three chapters outline the principles and practice of cultural intelligence and indicate how best to acquire it. Chapter 2 helps you to *understand* what cultural differences are and how they are reflected in different people's behavior. Chapter 3 helps you to *discard your assumptions* about the way people "should" behave, practice *mindfulness*—a kind of attention to culturally based behavior—and develop *behavioral skills* for use in cross-cultural situations. In Chapter 4 you will learn how to translate understanding, mindfulness, and behavioral skills into *action* and develop functioning cultural intelligence. The message in these chapters is that the task of understanding culture is not insurmountable, and if you learn the basic principles, adopt a mindful approach, and are prepared to act as a culturally adaptive person, you can function effectively in a variety of cross-cultural settings. Moreover, it will be a rewarding experience for you.

The subsequent five chapters apply the fundamentals of cultural intelligence to a number of common managerial challenges in multicultural settings. By applying the principles outlined you can be more effective in making decisions (Chapter 5), communicating and negotiating across cultures (Chapter 6), leading and motivating others who are culturally different (Chapter 7), designing, managing, and contributing to multicultural teams (Chapter 8), and in managing your international career (Chapter 9). The final chapter is a review and synthesis of the key learning points in the book. Finally, we provide a bibliography of key sources for those wanting to explore concepts in more depth.

As we wrote this book we were constantly reminded of our own cultural backgrounds. (Kerr is a Scot, who lives and works in New Zealand. Dave has New Zealand citizenship, but he was born and educated in the United States and now lives and works in Canada.) While we both have extensive international experience, and between us have lived and worked in ten different countries, we know that our cultural backgrounds influence our ability to be objective. We have worked very hard in this regard, but we would be pleased to hear from readers who feel we have missed or misinterpreted things that are obvious to them from their cultural perspective.

With this book we have attempted to write across cultural differences, to appreciate the wonderful diversity of our fellow human beings all around the world, and to help businesspeople everywhere become more knowledgeable, more attentive, and more skilled in their interactions with others. We sincerely believe that the widespread development of cultural intelligence would make the world, particularly the business world, a more productive and a happier place.

Dave Thomas,
Vancouver
March, 2004

Kerr Inkson,
Auckland
March, 2004

Acknowledgments

Along the path from book idea to final product, numerous individuals have influenced our work. Steve Piersanti at Berrett-Koehler helped to refine the concept for the book and has provided invaluable support and assistance throughout the process. Jeevan Sivasubramaniam, Managing Editor of Berrett-Koehler, did an expert job of guiding our journey. Though others at BK also deserve mention, including Michael Crowley, Dianne Platner and Rick Wilson, we thank everyone at BK for caring about our book and making it the best it could be. Katie Silver and her colleagues at BookMatters are responsible for fixing our sometimes suboptimal grammar and punctuation and also making the book pleasing to look at and easy to read. We are also grateful to Pillay Kriben, Jeffrey Kullick, John McIntyre, and Andrea Markowitz for their helpful comments on an early draft of the manuscript. Any errors and omissions are of course our responsibility alone.

Many of the ideas in this book were the product of, or refined in, numerous discussions that Dave has had with members of the International Organization Network (ION). A big Mango to you all! Iain Macfarlane provided Kerr with many helpful insights into life in international business. We are also very grateful to Richard Brislin for many of the examples of cross-cultural interactions that we have adapted for use here and to Bei Gong for researching the websites presented in the appendix.

Though the work on this book was accomplished largely by e-mail, we did collaborate in person for two weeks in Vancouver. During that time, Dave's partner, Tilley, not only tolerated two aging, obsessive-compulsive academics under her roof, she supported our efforts while also offering very valuable advice on the manuscript. Kerr is also indebted to his wife, Nan, for her unfailing support and love throughout the process. Both Tilley and Nan deserve more recognition than we can adequately express here.

This book is the product of a collaboration that began when Kerr recruited Dave to New Zealand in 1993. Little did we know then that many years (and a couple of countries) later we would be collaborating across thousands of kilometers on this project. In retrospect both of our experiences living and working in different cultures have had a dramatic influence on this volume. Our academic study has helped us make sense of the multicultural world around us, but it is the numerous cross-cultural interactions we have had that made culture "real" to us. We thank all those people who have helped to educate us and beg forgiveness from those we have offended along the way through our own lack of cultural intelligence.

CHAPTER 1

Are You a Global Manager?

Consider the following case study of Bill Miller, a global manager. Perhaps it is your story as well?

WHEN IS IT TIME TO DO BUSINESS?

Bill Miller, a top American salesman with a major information technology manufacturer, sits in his Mexico City hotel room, head bowed, running his hands through his hair in frustration. Will his hosts *ever* get down to talking business? Don't they know he has only a few days in their city? There is a deal to be made. The preliminary negotiations, conducted from a distance, have gone well. Yet, now, two days into his trip and with only twenty-four hours left, he feels he is no closer to "closing" than he was when he arrived.

It's not that his Mexican hosts are hostile. On the contrary, they are extraordinarily good-natured. They smile broadly at him, take a personal interest in him, and certainly look after all his physical needs; the hotel, for example, is excellent. It is just that the Mexicans show very little interest in talking business. The manager who has been assigned to look after Bill is a good host but is not party to the

1

deal Bill wants to negotiate. On the way in from the airport, when Bill brought up the subject of his sales presentation, which he had carefully prepared in the United States before the trip, the man seemed surprised that Bill wanted to talk about it. "Plenty of time for that later," he advised. "For the moment, you must be tired from your flight. Why not relax for a day or two and do some sightseeing first? I can look after you."

So Bill spent his first day being shown around Mexico City, struggling to conceal his impatience. On the second day, however, his host introduced him to the senior managers concerned with the proposed purchase and suggested that he make his presentation on the third morning. Again, they were very sociable, but seemed surprised at his impatience. Eventually they reluctantly agreed to an after-work discussion at 5:00 p.m.

Bill prepared carefully and arrived promptly at the meeting room with his PowerPoint display. There was no one there, just a cabinet of drinks and nibbles ready prepared. Gradually, however, the executives drifted in. They engaged Bill conversationally in English and began to ask questions. But the questions were not about the equipment Bill had to sell, but about his company—its history, its plans, and its future expansion in Latin America.

Next they moved on to Bill himself, his history in the company, his views of the I.T. industry and their own industry, his assessment of future economic policies, even his wife, family, and hobbies. Bill was still impatient. He wanted to get on with his presentation, but he did not want to offend his hosts, so he answered their questions and waited for a break in conversation. Eventually, during a pause, he said, "Thanks—I am so grateful for your hospitality. Now, I wonder if we might sit down and let me go through my presentation. I think we have a real good deal here for your company."

There was an embarrassed silence. Then the Deputy CEO said slowly, "Unfortunately, I think Mr. Alvarez may already have gone home." Sure enough, he had disappeared. Alvarez was the CEO, and without his signature there could be no deal. "Maybe . . ." said the deputy CEO, "maybe tomorrow? In the meantime, why not come out to dinner, so we can get to know each other better?" This time, Bill pleaded fatigue.

How on earth, he wondered, did these people ever sell anything to each other, or buy anything from each other, let alone from him?

■ ■ ■

Back at his home, Juan Alvarez lit a cigarette thoughtfully. The American had looked so ill at ease, so much a man in a hurry, that Juan just hadn't felt like sticking around. He had wanted to try to build a business relationship, establish the basis for many years' worth of deals, not just one. Miller had thrown it back in his face. Alvarez had seen it before with Americans.

How on earth, he wondered, did they ever learn to really trust each other in business?

The behavior of the different participants in the story and the reflections of Miller and Alvarez reveal quite distinct outlooks on business relationships and how best to pursue them. Bill, like most Americans, is concerned with getting things right in the short term, with being efficient, reaching agreement, and above all not wasting time. Juan and his staff, like members of most Latin cultures and many elsewhere in the world, believe that good business is the result of good business relationships. Therefore the initial effort must go into building a relationship: considered against the potential value of a long-term relationship, time is of little importance.

The result is that both Bill and Juan endanger what they value most—Bill endangers the immediate transaction and Juan endangers the long-term business relationship. If each had been willing to accommodate, at least in part, the other's customs—for example if Bill had allowed more time and had not let his impatience show, and if Juan had politely sat through Bill's presentation—a worthwhile business relationship could by now be under way. If either, or both, had learned the principles outlined in this book prior to Bill's visit it is likely that each could have secured exactly what he wanted.

The story of Bill Miller and Juan Alvarez is typical—it is a story that is enacted again and again in business negotiations around the world. Consider the following examples:

- A British company trying to run a Japanese subsidiary experiences inexplicable problems of morale and conflict with its Japanese workforce. This seems out of character with the usual politeness and teamwork of the Japanese. Later it is found that the British manager of the operation in Japan is not taken seriously because she is a woman.

- Two American managers meet with executives and engineers in a large Chinese electronics firm to present their idea for a joint venture. After several meetings they notice that different engineers seem to be attending the meetings and that their questions are becoming more technical, so much so that the Americans have difficulty answering them without giving away trade secrets. The Americans think this attempt to gain technological information is ridiculous. Don't the Chinese have any business ethics? How do they sleep at night? Later they learn that this is common practice and considered to be good business among the Chinese, who often suspect that Westerners are only interested in exploiting a cheap labor market.

- A Canadian manager faces difficulties because his five key subordinates are, respectively, French-Canadian, Indian, Italian-American, Chinese, and Iraqi. How can he treat them equitably? How can he find a managerial style that works with all of them? How should he chair meetings?

- An American couple about to take up a new assignment in Sri Lanka spend an evening visiting a Sri Lankan couple to whom they have been introduced by a friend. They want to "get a feel for" the Sri Lankan people. Their hosts are gracious and hospitable but much more reserved than the Americans are used to. The Americans feel awkward and find it hard to make conversation. Later, they panic because they realize how inept they felt in dealing with the Sri Lankans.[1]

These stories provide real-life examples of businesspeople from different parts of the world struggling with problems caused by intercultural differences. Do you identify with any of these situations? Do you wonder how to deal with people from other countries, cultures, or ethnic groups? Have you been in situations, like the ones above, that have left you puzzled and frustrated because you simply haven't felt tuned in to the people you have been dealing with? If so, then you are attempting to operate in a multicultural world.

The Global Village

There are seven billion people in the world from myriad different cultures, but we live in a village—the famed "global village" predicted by Marshall McLuhan[2] in the 1960s—where events taking place 10,000 miles away seem as close as events happening in the next street. We find ourselves in this global village whenever we read a newspaper or watch television. We can watch a Middle East firefight as if we were there.

On September 11, 2001, the world came to America, in a new and horrifying way. The young men who flew their hijacked airliners into the great U.S. citadels of the World Trade Center and the Pentagon were citizens of McLuhan's global village. They were operating in a world with a profoundly increased consciousness of difference—haves versus have-nots, Christians versus Muslims—as well as far fewer boundaries. To the terrorists, America was not a distant vision, but an outrage beamed nightly into their homes through their televisions, a place they could visit personally for the price of a plane ticket. They slipped easily into the world's greatest nation, acquired its language, were accepted by their neighbors, and took flying lessons from friendly, helpful locals. Most likely they tuned in to U.S. television at night and paid special attention to the regular bulletins on conflict in the Middle East.

The news of the attacks traveled, virtually instantaneously, to all corners of the globe. Californians stared aghast at the strange horrors of the day's breakfast show. Europeans interrupted their shopping to crowd around the television screens in appliance store windows. Australians phoned each other in the night and said, "switch your telly on." A billion viewers around the globe watched as the Twin Towers collapsed in front of their eyes.

The next day, we heard people say, "The world will never be the same again." What they might rather have said was, "The world has been changing rapidly for some time. This event has caused us to notice it."

After September 11, people struggled to understand. Who were these people who had plunged the world into crisis? Where were they from? What did they believe? What was it, in the ever more complicated cause-and-effect kaleidoscope of global economics and politics, that America had done to cause such bitter enmity among these terrorists and their supporters?

These events can only be understood if one takes a global perspective. These matters are not just about New York, or about America, or about the Middle East and its relationships with America. The forces involved are economic, political, legal, and cultural forces that cross international boundaries, create international problems, and require international solutions. We all see these things and, whether we like it or not, we are all involved. We are all citizens in a global world. And none of us can escape the fact.

Globalization of Business

We are all living increasingly global lives. But managers live lives that are more global than most. As the new century dawns we are beginning to see and understand the importance of the process known as globalization, and particularly the way it impacts the lives of people involved in business. Globalization means an increase in the permeability of traditional boundaries, including those around countries, economies, industries, and organizations.[3]

Globalization has recently been accelerated by a host of factors in the international business environment, including the following:

- new international trade agreements
- the growth of international trade
- the growth of multinational corporations
- the restructuring and downsizing of organizations
- the privatization of state enterprise
- the ability to locate business, particularly manufacturing, wherever cost is lowest
- the ability to execute financial transactions instantaneously on a global basis
- the transition of command economies to free markets
- the expansion of international migration
- the ability of information and communication technology to transcend time and distance

Although international commerce may have existed as early as 3000 B.C. it is only in the past few years that globalization has had such a broad effect on business. Until recently only a few very large multinational companies were concerned with foreign operations. For most firms business was largely local, tied closely to the city or region in which they were located, and certainly limited to the confines of the country. Now, business extends across all manner of porous boundaries—some of which have become so porous they have almost ceased to exist—across the entire globe. Even very small firms now have the capability to be global. With a computer, a modem, and a telephone connection it is possible to be a global business almost instantaneously. Because of globalization, the environment of business is now more complex, more dynamic, more uncertain, and more competitive than ever before. And there is no evidence that these trends will reverse or decrease.

Tomorrow's managers, even more than today's, will have to learn to compete, and to work, in a global world.

Globalization of People

Globalization is the result of dramatic shifts that have taken place in economics, politics, and technology. However, the day-to-day reality of global business involves interactions and relationships with people who are culturally different. In business today, we travel overseas among people from other cultures, we speak with them on international telephone calls, and we correspond with them by e-mail. Even in our home cities, we notice that more and more of our colleagues, our clients, and even the people we pass in the street are observably from cultures different from our own. The trend is inexorable. The range of different cultural backgrounds is huge; your colleagues, business associates, and contacts probably represent countries or ethnic groups from all over the world.

This globalization of people creates a new and major challenge for everyone who works in business. Although we increasingly cross boundaries and surmount barriers to trade, migration, travel, and the exchange of information, cultural boundaries are not so easily bridged. Unlike legal, political, or economic aspects of the business environment, which are observable, culture is largely invisible. Therefore, it is the aspect of global business that is most often overlooked.

The potential problems are enormous. Even when people come from the same culture, interpersonal skills are often poor, and this weakness is costly to business. Where interpersonal interaction is taking place across cultural boundaries, the potential for misunderstanding and failure is compounded.

The conclusion is clear. Whether you like it or not, you *are* a global manager. This is true, even if you have never done business abroad. You may never have gone around the globe, but the globe has come to you. Your company will most likely buy or sell abroad. Your company will be operating on a global stage or at least will be influenced by global events.

Here is a story about another global businessperson, this time one who has never left the shores of his own country:

THE JOB APPLICANT

In California, the human resource manager of a manufacturing company sits in his office. He is interviewing candidates for factory work, and the next candidate is due. Suddenly the door opens and a dark-skinned young man walks in. Without looking at the manager, the man finds the nearest chair, and, without waiting to be invited, he sits in it. He makes no eye contact with the manager but instead stares at the floor. The manager is appalled at such graceless behavior. The interview has not even started, and even though the jobs being filled do not require strong social skills, it is already unlikely that the young man will be appointed.

Observing this scene, most Americans might think that the human resource manager has come too quickly to a conclusion about a candidate who may have the potential to be a good worker, but they would fully understand why he felt as he did. The man's behavior certainly seems odd and disrespectful.

But suppose we add some new knowledge about the young man and his perspective on the interaction.

The young man is Samoan. He was born and brought up in Samoa and only recently immigrated to the United States. Samoans have great respect for authority, and the young man sees the manager as an important authority figure, deserving considerable respect. In Samoa you do not speak to, or even make eye contact with, authority figures until they invite you to do so. You do not stand while they are sitting, because to do so would put you on a physically higher level than they are, implying serious disrespect. In other words, in terms of his own cultural background and training, the young man has behaved exactly as he should. The human resource manager in the case above, if he himself were a job candidate, would greet his interviewer politely, make eye contact, offer a handshake, and wait to be invited to sit down. Therefore, he tends to expect similar behavior of everyone he interviews. In doing so, he is not only unfair to candidates who for various reasons operate differently, he also reduces his opportunity to benefit and learn from people from different cultural backgrounds.

We are all different, yet all too often we expect everyone else to be like us. If they don't do things the way we would do them, we assume there is something wrong with them. Why can't we think outside our little cultural rulebooks, accept and enjoy the wonderful diversity of humankind, and learn to work in harmony with others' ways?

In the cases we have provided so far, Bill and Juan and the human resource manager are playing a game that we all play. The game is called *Be Like Me*. Do it *my* way. Follow *my* rules. And, when the other party can't, or doesn't want to, Bill and Juan and the human resource manager withdraw into baffled incomprehension.

We all tend to be like Bill and Juan and the human resource manager. We all find cultural differences hard to deal with. We all tend to play *Be Like Me* with the people we live and work with.

Intercultural Failures

Many of us fail in intercultural situations in all sorts of ways, such as:

- Being unaware of the key features and biases of our own culture—not being able to see the forest because we are inside it! Remember that just as other cultures may seem odd to us, ours are just as odd to people from other cultures. For example, few Americans realize how *noisy* their natural extroversion and manner of conversation seem to those from most other cultures, many of which value reticence and modesty.

- Feeling threatened or uneasy when interacting with people who are culturally different. We may try not to be prejudiced against people from other cultures, but we notice, usually with tiny internal feelings of apprehension, the physical characteristics of others that make them different from us. All of us find difference threatening to some extent.

- Being unable to understand or explain the behavior of others who are culturally different. When we use a *Be Like Me* approach to explain the behavior of others we are often wrong because their behavior may not be based on the same goals or motives as ours.

- Being unable to transfer knowledge about one culture to another culture. Even people who have lots of travel experience in many different countries are often unable to use this experience to be more effective in each subsequent intercultural encounter.

- Not recognizing when our own cultural orientation is influencing our behavior. Much of our behavior is programmed by culture at a very deep level of consciousness and we are often unaware of this influence. Behavior that is normal to us may seem abnormal or even bizarre to culturally different others.

- Being unable to adjust to living and working in another culture. Anyone who has lived in a foreign culture for six months or more can attest to the difficulty in adjustment. The severity of culture shock may vary, but it affects us all.

In all of these examples, stress and anxiety for the manager is increased, and the end result is often impaired performance and lost business opportunities for the organization.

Ways of Overcoming Cultural Difference

If the above are the symptoms, what is the cure? How can ordinary people in business acquire the ability to feel at home when dealing with those from other cultures, to know what to say and do, and to pursue business relationships with the same degree of relaxation and the same expectation of synergy and success that they experience in relationships with others from their own culture?

One way of trying to deal with the problem is to stick to the *Be Like Me* policy and try to brazen it out. We can reason, particularly if we come from a dominating economy or culture, such as the United States, that it is for us to set norms for business behavior, and for others to learn how to imitate us.

Two arguments may be put forward in support of this position. First, it may be that a dominant culture will likely win in the end anyway. For example, the English language—the main language of North America and Britain but far from the most common language in the world—is becoming the lingua franca of business, is increasingly spoken in business circles all over Europe and large parts of Asia, and is being learned frantically by managers and aspiring managers everywhere.

Second, many people believe that cultures are converging to a common norm, assisted by phenomena such as mass communication and the standardization (or, as some call it, the McDonaldization) of consumption. Eventually, it is argued, the whole world will become like the United States anyway, and its citizens will think, talk, and act like Americans. Why resist the process?

In fact, as we will show in Chapter 2, the evidence in favor of "cultural convergence" is not compelling. Convergence is probably taking place only in superficial matters such as business procedures and consumer preferences. Also, insisting that other people behave as we do robs us of the great gift of diversity and the novelty it brings in the form of new ways of thinking and working. Finally, anyone who plays *Be Like Me* overtly or excessively is behaving insensitively and will be perceived as insensitive by others. Under these circumstances, any business opportunity will soon disappear.

UNDERSTANDING CULTURAL DIFFERENCES

Can we solve the problem of cultural differences simply by learning what other cultures are like? Do we even know, in any organized way, what they are like?

There is plenty of easily accessible information about other cultures. Cultural anthropologists have researched many of the cultures and subcultures of the world. And cultural differences among businesspeople have been explored by other academics.[4] This information has been useful in establishing the normative behavior or cultural stereotypes of many national cultures. It provides a starting point for anticipating culturally based behavior.

Understanding some of the key dimensions of cultural difference, some of the main differences between different countries in respect of these dimensions, and how they are manifested in business behavior is an important first step to cultural intelligence. This book provides some basic information on these matters.

However, this basic knowledge is only the beginning of overcoming cultural differences. Even at their best, research on cultural difference and the sort of account that says, "Japanese behave in this way and Americans in that" can provide only a very broad statement about cultural identity. The generalizations about a country are likely to conceal huge variances within that country and considerable subtlety in the way cultural differences are made apparent. There are likely to be, for example, religious or tribal or ethnic differences, detailed forms of special protocol, and regional variations.

The "laundry-list" approach to cross-cultural understanding attempts to provide each manager who is to have intercultural business interactions with a list—"everything you need to know"—about the particular country. Such lists attempt to detail not just what the key cultural characteristics are, but the regional or organizational variations, the expected behavior in that country, the detailed customs to be followed, the type of speech inflections to use, and expressions and actions that might be considered offensive, as well as functional information on matters such as living costs, health services, and education. You can buy books of this type about most countries, and some companies preparing executives for an expatriate assignment take this approach to preparing their prospective assignees and their families for the transition.

Laundry lists have their place, but they are cumbersome. They have to document every trait of every conceivable cultural variant, along with drills and routines to cater for each. For an expatriate, this kind of intensive preparation for a single defined destination may be highly appropriate, but for most of us our engagement with other cultures is a less intensive interaction with a variety of cultures. If we are traveling in, or entertaining business visitors from, half a dozen contrasting countries, do we have to learn an elaborate laundry list for each one? If we are suddenly introduced to culturally different people without warning, and have no laundry list readily available, how can we cope with the situation?

Furthermore, laundry lists tend to be rather dry and formal. The essence of culture is subtler, and it is hard to express in print. Formal and abstract knowledge needs to be supplemented by and integrated with experience of the culture. Learning facts about other cultures is by itself nowhere near enough.

BECOMING CULTURALLY INTELLIGENT

A third approach to the problem is to become culturally intelligent.[5]

Cultural intelligence means being skilled and flexible about understanding a culture, learning more about it from your ongoing interactions with it, and gradually reshaping your thinking to be more sympathetic to the culture and your behavior to be more skilled and appropriate when interacting with others from the culture.

Culturally intelligent people are like the ancient Greek Proteus. Proteus was a supernatural character in Homer's *Odyssey,* a sea dweller who could change shape at will and become a fish, or a lion, or a tree, or a fire. This adaptation was guided by knowledge and mindfulness of his situation. The global manager of today and tomorrow must learn to be like Proteus—flexible enough to adapt with knowledge and sensitivity to each new cultural situation that he or she faces.

Cultural intelligence has three parts.

- First, the culturally intelligent manager requires *knowledge* of culture and of the fundamental principles of cross-cultural interactions. This means knowing what culture is, how cultures vary, and how culture affects behavior.

- Second, the culturally intelligent manager needs to practice *mindfulness*, the ability to pay attention in a reflective and creative way to cues in the cross-cultural situations encountered.

- Third, based on knowledge and mindfulness, the culturally intelligent manager develops *behavioral skills*, and becomes competent across a wide range of situations. These skills involve choosing the appropriate behavior from a well-developed repertoire of behaviors that are correct for different intercultural situations.

The model in Figure 1.1 is a graphic representation of cultural intelligence.

As shown, each element is interrelated with the other. As we describe in Chapter 4, the process of becoming culturally intelligent involves a cycle or repetition in which each new challenge is built upon until cultural intelligence is ultimately achieved. A major advantage of this approach over the laundry-list approach is that as well as acquiring growing competence

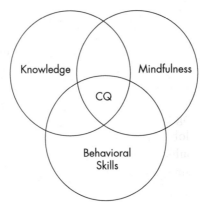

FIGURE 1.1. Components of cultural intelligence (CQ)

in a specific culture you simultaneously acquire general cultural intelligence, making each new cultural challenge easier to face because of what has been learned from the previous ones.

You have probably heard of the psychologists' concept of intelligence, the ability to reason, and its measure, the intelligence quotient (IQ). More recently has come recognition that it is important how we handle our emotions, captured by the concept called emotional intelligence, measured by a questionnaire giving an emotional intelligence quotient (EQ). Cultural intelligence (or CQ as its measure would be called[6]) is a relatively new idea that builds on these earlier concepts, but that incorporates the capability to interact effectively across cultures.

The concept of cultural intelligence as outlined in this book is not difficult to understand but is hard to put into practice on an ongoing basis. It takes time and effort to develop a high CQ and the concomitant skills. Years of studying, observing, reflecting, and experimenting lie ahead before the manager is likely to develop truly skilled performance. Becoming culturally intelligent is substantially learning by doing, so it has useful outcomes beyond the development of skilled intercultural performance. In addition, new cultures are intriguing, and learning how to work in them can be a lot of fun. This book is the place to start on this journey.

Summary

This chapter describes the forces of globalization that are dramatically changing the environment for businesspeople around the globe. The global manager is no longer just the jet-setting international troubleshooter or seasoned expatriate manager. We are all becoming global managers, for even those who stay in their own countries have to think in global terms and interact with those from other cultures. The essence of being global is interacting with people who are culturally different. Culture is more difficult to deal with than other aspects of the business environment, partly because much of culture operates invisibly. We know a great deal about how cultures around the world differ. However, this knowledge is only the beginning to becoming culturally intelligent. Cultural intelligence involves understanding the fundamentals of intercultural interaction, developing a mindful approach to intercultural interactions, and finally building adaptive skills and a repertoire of behaviors so that one is effective in different intercultural situations. Interacting effectively across cultures is now a fundamental requirement in today's global business environment.

CHAPTER 2

Understanding Culture: What Culture Is and Is Not

Chan Yuk Fai had ushered his British guest into the crowded Shanghai restaurant. Around them, the atmosphere was busy with the quiet babble of a dozen conversations. Mr. Chan bowed slightly, then leaned forward and smiled.

"I think," he said in excellent English, "I think the food is not the very best in this restaurant."

Jeffrey Thomson stiffened slightly. He found it hard to conceal his surprise. What was he to make of Mr. Chan's remark? Mr. Chan had chosen the restaurant. Did he really think the food was poor? If he thought so, why had he chosen that restaurant? Perhaps criticizing the food was just a Chinese custom—something everyone did that had nothing to do with the real quality of the food. Perhaps it was a joke—after all, Mr. Chan was smiling broadly. After all, what did he know about the Chinese sense of humor? Or perhaps it was an affectation of modesty. He had read somewhere that Chinese were self-effacing. But he had also read that they were indirect. Maybe criticizing the restaurant was Mr. Chan's way of saying he did not have a lot of interest in the business deal they had come to the restaurant to discuss. Maybe it was even some form of veiled insult!

He realized that Mr. Chan was politely waiting for him to respond and that he had no idea what to say. He felt very confused. Best to be noncommittal, he thought. What would I say if someone said that to me in London? He smiled back at him.

"I'm sure we can make the best of it," he replied.

Was it his imagination, or did he see a minuscule reduction in Mr. Chan's beaming smile?[1]

On the surface Jeffrey Thomson's worries about Chinese culture have to do with Chinese customs, the habitual ways in which people go about day-to-day activities. It is customary in China to show respect for a guest by disparaging one's own accomplishments, even the selection of a restaurant. And, there is an expectation that the guest will return this respect with a compliment. By not doing so Jeffery has made a cultural blunder. This custom is specific to the cultural situation, but the general predicament in which Jeffery finds himself is one which he has in common with thousands of other travelers from all continents and countries. He lacks cultural intelligence.

Components of Cultural Intelligence

Jeffrey's problem can be divided into three linked components.

First, he lacks detailed *knowledge*. He understands that there are such things as cross-cultural differences. His mind has retained a few ideas (from where, who knows?) about characteristics of Chinese people like the man he is dealing with. But these are crude stereotypes that leave open multiple interpretations and are of little help in enabling him to understand the situation.

Second, he lacks what we call *mindfulness*. Not only does he not know what Mr. Chan's remark means, but he lacks the ability to observe and interpret the remark in the context of other cues—prior conversations, his dealings with other Chinese, Mr. Chan's smile, and so on. Because of this, he is unable to read the situation as it develops. Whatever the outcome, he is likely to learn little from the experience that will assist him with further interactions. Mindfulness is a means of observing and understanding cultural meanings and using that understanding as a basis for immediate action and long-term learning.

Third, he lacks the skill to adapt his *behavior*. He would love to be able to respond confidently, in both his words and his physical actions, in a way that would be authentic but also sensitive to his host. He realizes that being able to respond in the correct way to Mr. Chan's remark would not only put both himself and his host more at ease, but also help their substantive business conversation. But the only action he is capable of—due in part to his lack of knowledge and in part to his lack of interpretive skills—is to respond, as he would do "at home." Jeffrey needs to develop a repertoire of behaviors that will enable him to act appropriately and successfully in any cross-cultural situation.

The three components combined provide a template for intercultural flexibility and competence. In brief, culturally intelligent people have:

- the *knowledge* to understand cross-cultural phenomena
- the *mindfulness* to observe and interpret particular situations
- the skill of adapting *behavior* to act appropriately and successfully in a range of situations

These three components are connected to and build on each other. Because culturally intelligent people have good background understanding, their interpretation is assisted—they know what to look for. But each competency is also based on wider characteristics that we all have to different degrees: those who find cultural intelligence easiest to acquire are people who are interested in novel learning and social interaction and who already have good communication skills. For those who are unsure of themselves in these areas, acquiring cultural intelligence is also likely to increase competence and confidence in *all* interpersonal situations.

In this and the next two chapters, we present a road map for improving your cultural intelligence by addressing the three issues one by one.

In this chapter we look at the information base that supports the necessary background understanding of cultural phenomena. A secure *knowledge* of what culture is and what it is not, of the depth, strength, and shared and systematic nature of culture, and of some of the main types of cultural difference provides a good basic set of tools to give confidence in any cross-cultural situation.

In Chapter 3 we consider how observation of the everyday behavior of people from different backgrounds—including our own behavior—can be useful in interpreting the frameworks of knowledge introduced in this chapter. Most people operate interpersonally in a condition of "cruise control," in which their experiences are interpreted from the standpoint of their own culture. We develop the idea of *mindfulness*—a process of observing and reflecting that incorporates cross-cultural knowledge. Developing the habit and the techniques of mindfulness is a key means to improving cultural intelligence. We then outline the process through which knowledge and mindfulness lead to new *behavioral skills*. The behavioral skills associated with cultural intelligence are general skills that are derived from specific knowledge. By developing this repertoire of behavior, you can translate the understanding of culture into effective cross-cultural interactions. In Chapter 4 we show how a functioning cultural intelligence is developed. Because characteristics such as integrity, openness, and hardiness support the development of a high CQ, everyone can learn to be more culturally intelligent.

In the case study that opened this chapter, a culturally intelligent Jeffrey would have been mindfully aware of Mr. Chan's remarks and would have adapted his behavior by choosing from a number of more appropriate responses. But in order to do this Jeffrey would have had to have a basic understanding of culture.

What Culture Is

Culture is a word that is familiar to everyone, but its precise meaning can be elusive. A useful definition by noted social scientist Geert Hofstede[2] is that culture consists of shared mental programs that condition individuals' responses to their environment. This simple definition neatly encapsulates the idea that we *see* culture in everyday behavior—individuals' responses to their environment, such as Chan Yuk Fai's and Jeffrey Thomson's efforts at conversation—but that such behavior is controlled by deeply embedded mental programs. Culture is not just a set of surface behaviors, it is deeply embedded in each of us. The surface features of our social behavior—for example, our mannerisms, our ways of speaking to each other, the way we dress—are often manifestations of deep culturally based values and principles.

A key feature of culture is that these mental programs are shared—Chan Yuk Fai and Jeffrey Thomson share theirs with many other people from their own ethnic or national communities. Hofstede talks about three different levels of mental programming, shown in Figure 2.1.

- The deepest level—*human nature*—is based on common biological reactions such as hunger, sexual drive, territoriality, and nurturing of the young, which all members of the human race have in common. Because of human nature, there are many behaviors and understandings that all people share, even though they come from different cultures.

- The shallowest level—*personality*—is based on the specific genetic makeup and personal experiences that make each of us a unique individual—for example, we may be sociable or introverted, aggressive or submissive, emotional or stable,

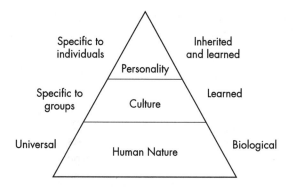

FIGURE 2.1. Three levels of mental programming

or perhaps, as a result of learning, have a deep interest in model railways or a love of good wine. Because of personality, there are many behaviors and understandings that will be quite different between different people even though they come from the same culture.

- The middle level—*culture*—is based on common experiences that we share with a particular group of our fellow human beings. Cultural values, attitudes, and behavior give us something in common with a definable group of others, but not with all of them. The group may be a very large one, such as a national population, for example, Japanese culture; or a very small one, for example, the culture of the committee of a local PTA.[3] In recent years, many business organizations have recognized the power of culture to shape individual values and actions and have worked hard to establish "organizational cultures" that will bond the activities of diverse members to common values and themes such as customer service or excellence.[4]

In this book we are concerned mostly with the larger cultural issues of national or ethnic culture. But the notion of smaller cultures—sometimes referred to as subcultures—and the idea of individual personality remind us that within any given culture there is huge variation and that one of the biggest barriers to effective intercultural interaction is basing our behavior on stereotypes, which assume that all members of a given culture are identical.

Characteristics of Culture

There are some basic characteristics that apply to any culture, which are worth keeping in mind.

CULTURE IS SHARED

By definition, culture is something that a group has in common that is not normally available to people outside the group. It is mental programming held in common that enables insiders to interact with each other with a special intimacy denied outsiders.

For example, Scottish people all over the world share an understanding of history that is rooted in conflict with, and oppression by, the English. Even though the two groups nowadays operate relatively harmoniously, this simple fact creates a bond among Scots and an attitude toward the English that is hard to put into words but is immediately recognized by Scottish people when they meet anywhere in the world.

CULTURE IS LEARNED AND IS ENDURING

The example of the Scots and the English tells us that culture does not arise by accident, but builds up systematically over time. The mental programming of a group is learned by its members over long periods as they interact with their environment. Some aspects of culture are built into institutions, such as religious beliefs, systems of land ownership, forms of marriage, and the like. Others are passed on through the generations in the form of parental role-modeling and advice to the young.

CULTURE IS A POWERFUL INFLUENCE ON BEHAVIOR

It is hard for us to escape our culture, even when we want to. The mental programming involved is strong. Even when we mentally question the rationality of some aspects of our culture or seek to adopt cultural flexibility by doing things in line with a different culture, we have a natural tendency to revert to our cultural roots.

One of the authors knew a young man brought up in a strict Christian culture that taught him that the theater is the house of the Devil. On going to university and mixing with more liberal people, he decided that from a rational point of view there was nothing wrong with going to the theater. But on his first visit, he became nauseous and had to leave to be sick. His culture had programmed him extremely powerfully. To some extent this book, in encouraging cultural flexibility in cross-cultural situations, is asking readers to try to do something that may not come naturally.

Nevertheless, the experience of migrants, who deliberately and often successfully move from one cultural setting to another, suggests that it is quite possible for individuals to lose aspects of their old cultures and to learn new ones particular to their new environment. This happens through a process known as acculturation.[5] Being embedded in an unfamiliar setting causes some to learn actively about the new culture, while others attempt to avoid it, often by trying to recreate their old culture in the new situation. The best adaptation is done by those who learn the new culture while still retaining valuable elements of their home culture. By so doing, they cultivate the cultural intelligence that we advocate in this book.

CULTURE IS SYSTEMATIC AND ORGANIZED

Culture is not random. It is an organized system of values, attitudes, beliefs, and meanings that are related to each other and to the environmental context. To understand why Chan Yuk

Fai says, "I think the food is not the very best in this restaurant," it is not sufficient to understand that Chinese people often deprecate their own food. We need to understand that such deprecation is but one tiny expression of a complex system of values and ideas. It is a surface representation of Mr. Chan's deepest values and understanding of the world—a mental program based on centuries of survival and cooperation by Mr. Chan's Chinese ancestors in their largely agricultural economy and culture. As another example, the practice of polygamy, which is frowned on in most cultures, makes good historical sense in some African cultures where it is still practiced. It depends on such factors as family status, economic security, and religious commitment, all of which are based on having more children, and particularly more sons, per family.

Because of the mental programming imposed by our own culture, the cultures of other people often seem strange and illogical. Deeper scrutiny can reveal that each culture has its own, often exquisite, logic and coherence.

CULTURE IS LARGELY INVISIBLE

What we see of culture is expressed in living artifacts. These include communicated messages such as that of Mr. Chan concerning the food. But they also include human activities like language, customs, and dress, as well as physical artifacts such as architecture, art, and decoration.

However, much of culture is hidden. These obvious and visible elements of culture may be likened to the tip of an iceberg.[6] (Icebergs have as much as 90 percent of their mass below the surface of the water, leaving only a small percentage visible.) The important part of this particular iceberg is not the obvious physical symbols that are above the surface, but the deep underlying values and assumptions that they express. So, understanding cultures involves a lot more than just understanding immediate surface behavior such as bows, handshakes, invitations, ceremonies, and body language. It is the invisible elements of culture—for example, the underlying values, social structures, and ways of thinking—that are most important.

CULTURE MAY BE "TIGHT" OR "LOOSE"

Cultures differ from each other not just in their details, but also in their pervasiveness.[7] In some societies there is virtually 100 percent agreement as to the form of correct behavior; in others there may be much greater diversity and tolerance of difference. "Tight" cultures have uniformity and agreement and are often based on homogeneous populations or the dominance of particular religious beliefs. Japan is a good example. Countries such as the United States with diverse populations have relatively "loose" cultures, which are made even looser in some cases by the encouragement of freedom of thought and action.

National and Global Culture

As we have mentioned, nation and culture are not identical. Many ethnic cultures, organizational cultures, minority cultures, and subcultures may influence different people within the same country. For example, the First Nations peoples of the United States and Canada have distinctive cultural characteristics very different from those of the majority of American and Canadian citizens, and both countries have many distinctive cultural groupings within their populations. The main focus of this book is on national culture.

Nations are often formed because of cultural similarities among different population groups, and over time they reinforce their adherence to a national culture by means of shared institutions, legal and educational systems, and of course, nowadays, the mass media. National cultures are particularly important in international business because of the concept of national sovereignty and the need to conduct business affairs within national, legal, and political frameworks.

Another issue regarding national culture concerns the apparent growth of "global culture." Some people argue that the effect of the internationalization of travel, business, and the media is to make all countries converge toward a single culture, ironing out all the special differences that make each national culture and subculture unique. Because of the economic dominance of Western countries, particularly the United States and the larger European democracies, it is thought by some that these countries' cultural forms will gradually submerge cultures around the world. Thus, the international proliferation of organizations such as McDonald's and Starbucks are often welcomed as economic success stories but also criticized as an intrusion of American culture.

If the convergence theory is correct, it might be a reason to downplay the notion of cultural intelligence. If this is the case, it could be best to work with people from all nations to help them to get away from their own cultural habits and instead to understand and practice the values and customs that are becoming standard around the world.

We think that this is a bad strategy for three reasons:

1. While there is some evidence to support the convergence theory, there is other evidence to oppose it.[8] While all cultures may be becoming "modern" they are doing so in different ways. Cultures tend to accept some aspects of other societies and reject others. In Hong Kong, for example, people have retained their traditional Chinese respect for authority while rejecting its fatalism and have adopted modern competitiveness but rejected modern attitudes toward sexual promiscuity. Overall, probably the only real convergence that is taking place is in surface matters such as basic business structures and consumer preferences, rather than in fundamental ways of thinking and behavior.

2. Even if convergence is taking place, the pace of change is very slow. The evolution of culture in any society is not easily predicted. Traditional cultural patterns tend to be deeply

embedded. Those who intend to sit back and wait for the rest of the world to catch up with the West in terms of culture will have to wait for a very long time.

3. There is increasing recognition worldwide of the value of diversity in human affairs. Just as biodiversity has a value in allowing ecosystems to deal with major change, so too does cultural diversity offer us a wider range of viewpoints and ways of doing things. Most societies nowadays go out of their way to ensure that cultures under threat are protected from submergence by majority cultures. Business needs to think in a similar manner.

Key Cultural Values

In Chapter 1, we rejected the laundry-list approach to understanding cultures—learning everything one needs to know about every culture one is likely to deal with—on the basis that cultures are so diverse and so complex that the task is impossible.

Nevertheless it *is* possible to "unpackage" cultures by describing their essential features in order to assist understanding. It is a bit like the language we use to describe people. Sally may be a unique individual with specific qualities and quirks of character that would take a long time to describe. But if we say Sally is intelligent, extroverted, emotionally stable, and unassertive we have in a few words conveyed a lot of information about Sally that might differentiate her from other people.

Just as we can summarize people's individual characteristics, we can summarize the characteristics of a culture. An important way to describe both the similarities and differences among cultures is by their underlying values. These cultural values are fundamental shared beliefs about how things should be or how one should behave.

Consider the case below.

David Taylor, an American student studying Chinese in Taiwan, met Chen Li-Men, a young man from Taipei, at a local food stand. Chen Li-Men, anxious to have a foreign acquaintance and perhaps practice some English, struck up a conversation. David also wanted to familiarize himself with Chinese cultural norms and to experience the local lifestyle. As the two were talking, David mentioned his interest in the outdoors: climbing, hiking, and camping. Chen Li-Men suggested that they go hiking together in the nearby mountains, just outside the city, and promised to arrange everything. David, who was looking forward to getting to know someone who could give him some insights into the culture, as well as having some time away from the noise and congestion of the city, readily agreed. When they finally met to go hiking, however, they were greeted by some of Li-Men's friends, the whole group numbering around twenty-five. Many were anxious to talk to David. David, though visibly disappointed, said nothing, but tended to withdraw from the rest of the group. Chen Li-Men noticed his reclusive behavior and was bewildered. He could not understand why, when he had gone to such lengths to call his friends and arrange everything, David was still not pleased.[9]

The explanation for this cross-cultural misunderstanding is based on an important dimension of value variation between cultures. Chinese have a much more group-oriented culture than Americans. When an activity is planned, it is much more common to invite a large group than just one or two others. These differentiating factors are called *individualism* and *collectivism*.

- In *individualistic* cultures people are most concerned about the consequences of action for themselves, not others. They prefer activities conducted on one's own or in relatively private interactions with friends. Decisions are made by the individual according to the judgment he or she makes as to what is appropriate and the individual rewards that will accrue.

- In *collectivistic* cultures, people primarily view themselves as members of groups and collectives rather than as autonomous individuals. They are concerned about the effects of actions on their groups. Their activities are more likely to be taken in groups on a more public basis. Decisions are made on a consensus or consultative basis, and the effects of the decision on everyone in the social group are taken into account.

Individualism and collectivism are not either-or. They are dimensions along which different cultures can be arranged.

HOFSTEDE'S STUDY

In Geert Hofstede's well-known survey of over 100,000 employees of a large multinational corporation spread across fifty countries, each country, on the basis of its employees' responses, was assigned an individualism score between 1 and 100.[10] The most individualistic countries on this measure were Australia, Belgium, Canada, Great Britain, Italy, New Zealand, South Korea, and the United States, all of which had scores of over 75. Countries that scored less than 20 included Columbia, Costa Rica, El Salvador, Guatemala, Indonesia, Pakistan, Panama, Peru, Taiwan, and Venezuela. The countries with high scores were all North American, European, or former colonies of the United Kingdom. The lower scores were found in countries based in South America and East Asia. Among countries that came out around the average for individualism-collectivism were Argentina, India, Japan, and Spain.

It is easy to see how it might be difficult for individuals from one group of countries to know how to behave socially in the other or to understand the process of making decisions in the other. Consider again the case, described in Chapter 1, of the individualistic American Bill Miller trying to cut a deal in collectivist Latin America.

Individualism-collectivism, while perhaps the most important

TABLE 2.1   Hofstede's index

COUNTRY	POWER DISTANCE	INDIVIDUALISM	MASCULINITY	UNCERTAINTY AVOIDANCE
Argentina	49	46	56	86
Australia	36	90	61	51
Austria	11	55	79	70
Belgium	65	75	54	94
Brazil	69	38	49	76
Canada	39	80	52	48
Chile	63	23	28	86
Colombia	67	13	64	80
Costa Rica	35	15	21	86
Denmark	48	74	16	23
Equador	78	8	63	67
Finland	33	63	26	59
France	68	71	43	86
Germany (F.R.)	35	67	66	65
Great Britain	35	89	66	35
Greece	60	35	57	112
Guatemala	95	6	37	101
Hong Kong	68	25	57	29
Indonesia	78	14	46	48
India	77	48	56	40
Iran	58	41	43	59
Ireland	28	70	68	35
Israel	13	54	47	81
Italy	50	76	70	75
Jamaica	45	39	68	13
Japan	54	46	95	92
Korea (S)	60	18	39	85

(continued)

TABLE 2.1 *(continued)*

COUNTRY	POWER DISTANCE	INDIVIDUALISM	MASCULINITY	UNCERTAINTY AVOIDANCE
Malaysia	104	26	50	36
Mexico	81	30	69	82
Netherlands	38	80	14	53
Norway	31	69	8	50
New Zealand	22	79	58	49
Pakistan	55	14	50	70
Panama	95	11	44	86
Peru	64	16	42	87
Philippines	94	32	64	44
Portugal	63	27	31	104
South Africa	49	65	63	49
Salvador	66	19	40	94
Singapore	74	20	48	8
Spain	57	51	42	86
Sweden	31	71	5	29
Switzerland	34	68	70	58
Taiwan	58	17	45	69
Thailand	64	20	34	64
Turkey	66	37	45	85
Uruguay	61	36	38	100
United States	40	91	62	46
Venezuela	81	12	73	76
Yugoslavia	76	27	21	88
Regions:				
East Africa	64	27	41	52
West Africa	77	20	46	54
Arab countries	80	38	53	68

Source: Adapted from Hofstede (1980)

dimensions of cultural variation are not the only dimensions of culture that researchers have been able to identify. For example, in Hofstede's study mentioned previously, three other factors were identified.

- *Power distance:* the extent to which large differentials of power, for example between a boss and a subordinate or between a higher-status and a lower-status person, are expected and tolerated. Autocratic behavior by a boss would be much better tolerated in a high power distance country.

- *Uncertainty avoidance:* the extent to which the culture emphasizes focusing on ways to reduce uncertainty and create stability—for example, having clear written rules and procedures or strong norms to guide action. Formal organizational procedures may be much more necessary in a high uncertainty avoidance country.

- *Masculinity/femininity:* the balance between the traditional "male" goals of ambition and achievement and "female" orientations to nurturance and interpersonal harmony—for example, the balance between seeking promotion at work and having good relationships with others.

Hofstede's complete rankings are shown in Table 2.1. We encourage you to spend a few minutes looking at this table and thinking about what it says. In particular, focus on your own country, check its figures, and consider whether the story they tell squares with your experience. If necessary, go back and reread the definitions we have provided of the various dimensions. Also consider other countries that you know, or have an idea about. Spending a little time on this exercise may markedly increase your background awareness.

SCHWARTZ VALUE SURVEY

Shalom Schwartz[11] and his colleagues did a more recent and more sophisticated mapping of cultures according to their value orientations. They identified three universal human re-

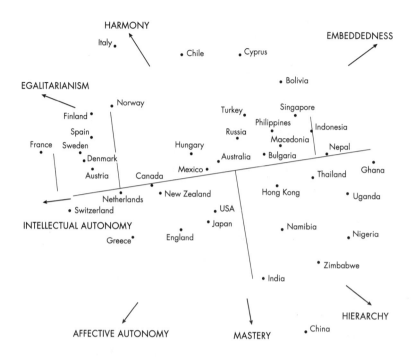

FIGURE 2.2. Co-plot of value dimensions across national cultures.
Source: Adapted from Sagiv & Schwartz, 2000

quirements. The first was the nature of the relationship of the individual to the group. The second was the preservation of society itself. The final issue was people's relationship to the natural world. Their idea was that while all societies have to address these same issues, they do so in different ways. This leads to different cultural values or a shared set of fundamental beliefs about how things should be or how one should behave. By examining fifty-seven national cultures, seven of these fundamental value dimensions were derived:

- Egalitarianism—Recognition of people as moral equals
- Harmony—Fitting in harmoniously with the environment
- Embeddedness—People as part of a collective

- Hierarchy—Unequal distribution of power
- Mastery—Exploitation of the natural or social environment
- Affective autonomy—Pursuit of positive experiences
- Intellectual autonomy—Independent pursuit of own ideas

Figure 2.2 shows the relative position of countries along the seven dimensions.

It is impossible to perfectly represent the relative position of countries on seven dimensions in the two-dimensional space of the printed page. However, by using a technique called a co-plot, we are able to present the relationships quite accurately. The position of each country along the vector of each cultural dimension indicates how similar or different each country is on that dimension. For example, Canada and New Zealand are very similar on all seven dimensions. However, the United States, which is similar to these two countries on other dimensions, ranks higher on the mastery dimension (more like Japan). As with Hofstede's numerical comparisons, examining the position of your own country and that of others on this map can increase your knowledge about the areas of potential agreement and disagreement with members of another culture.

INDIVIDUALISM AND COLLECTIVISM

Of all the dimensions established by Hofstede, Schwartz and others, the most useful and powerful are individualism and collectivism.[12] However, it is important not to simplify these dimensions, by equating individualism with selfishness or introversion, for example, or collectivism with socialism. Both individualists and collectivists have relationships and groups, but the type of relationship is different: collectivists actually tend to have fewer groups with which they identify, but these are wide, diverse groups such as tribes or organizations, and the bonds of loyalty are strong. Individualists often identify with many different groups, but the bonds are superficial.

As we have shown, individualism is most common in developed Western countries. There is a strong relationship between a country's individualism and its wealth (GNP).[13] The recent political fashion of free markets and the encouragement of entrepreneurship plays to individualism, and in developed countries there has been a marked international trend in this direction, leading, for example, to a general decline in individuals' loyalty to their employing organizations. Such forces can threaten the social fabric of a country because of the threat to its cultural values or may increase the differences between cultures as they change at different rates.

Effects of Culture: The "In-group" and the "Out-group"

An important aspect of culture is the way we use it to define ourselves. If we state that we are "American," "Thai," "Muslim," or that we "work for IBM," our assertion places us inside a boundary that excludes a lot of others. It differentiates us. It sets up expectations—intentional or unintentional—as to the kinds of attitudes and behavior that others can expect from us.

This has particular importance in terms of bias—typically bias is in favor of our own group or culture (the "in-group"), and against others (the "out-group") external to our own. Therefore, we typically discriminate in our own group's favor.

Most importantly, we tend to identify everything about the in-group as being normal (i.e., the way things ought to be done). Consequently, whenever we encounter people doing things a different way, we tend to see their action not just as different, but as deviant, even as wrong. We are particularly likely to do this when operating on our own turf, within the boundaries of our own group or culture. We tend to believe that "when in Rome, you do as the Romans do," yet even when we are overseas, like Jeffrey Thomson in the opening case, we tend to take our own common experiences at home as the norm for how others ought to behave in their country.

For example, Hofstede's research shows that although the

United States and Guatemala are geographically close to each other, they are widely separated by cultural distance. On a scale with a mean of 50 points, Hofstede scored the two countries as follows:

HOFSTEDE DIMENSION	U.S.A.	GUATEMALA
Individualism	91	6
Power distance	40	95
Masculinity	62	37
Uncertainty avoidance	46	101

From the table, it is apparent that the United States has a very high level of individualism, above average masculinity, and moderate power distance and uncertainty avoidance. Guatemala, on the other hand, has very low individualism, very high power distance, below average masculinity, and very high uncertainty avoidance.

Consider how an American and a Guatemalan, each with no prior cross-cultural experience, might perceive each other from the standpoint of their own cultures. Despite some extreme scores in both countries, individuals from each are likely to judge the other as though his or her own country represents the norm. Each will take "the way we do things at home" as a starting point. The American may find irritating the Guatemalans' emphasis on social activity, the slowness of their consultative decision making, the autocracy of their high-status people and the obsequiousness of their low-status people, their softness, and their discomfort with any sort of ambiguity or with taking decisive action on their own initiative. For their part, the Guatemalans might see the Americans as being self-centered, over-familiar, aggressive, and anarchical.

For this reason, the first step to cultural flexibility is to *understand your own culture* and how it affects your interpretation of the behavior of others. This is an important part—though far from the only part—of the cultural makeup and stereotyping that you most likely bring to each new cross-cultural situation you face. We have already suggested that you locate your own culture in terms of the Hofstede data and/or the Schwartz map. Think about it again in terms of all its special features and idiosyncrasies. Try to look at it through the eyes of people from contrasting cultures.

Summary

This chapter describes how knowledge of what culture is and how it varies and affects behavior is the first stage of developing cultural intelligence. Culture is not a random assortment of customs and behaviors. It is the values, attitudes, and assumptions about behavior that are shared by people in specific groups. It is systematic and organized and has developed as a result of societies' learning to deal with their common problems. Cultures can be defined according to their values—the fundamental beliefs that people within the culture share about how things should be and how one should behave. Culture is shared; it is passed on from one generation to the next. While it has a profound influence on behavior, the most important aspects of culture are invisible. A key feature of culture is that it categorizes others and us into in-groups and out-groups. This categorization of people into "them and us" underlies much cross-cultural behavior. There are several important dimensions along which cultures can be defined, the most important being individualism and collectivism. By understanding our own culture we can then make initial comparisons with others to understand areas of possible agreement or disagreement. The knowledge gained in this way is a necessary first step to becoming culturally intelligent. In subsequent chapters we link this knowledge with the important elements of mindfulness and adaptive skills.

CHAPTER 3

Switching Off
Cultural Cruise Control

THE TRADE PERMIT

Mohammed is an immigration official in a Middle Eastern country. One of his jobs is to review applications for trading permits issued to overseas visitors. He has to ensure that all the appropriate criteria are met. If they are, he will normally grant the permit.

Mohammed's salary for this job is extremely low. Relying on his salary alone, Mohammed would find it very difficult to provide even the bare essentials for his family. Fortunately there is relief for him in the system: he is good at his job, and it is customary for applicants to show their appreciation for his service by giving him small sums of money. Some of these applicants are Americans and Europeans from wealthy multinational companies, which can easily afford these additional costs. The arrangement is well understood by nearly everyone in Mohammed's country and works to the advantage of all.

Recently, however, Mohammed has had some difficulty working with a man called John O'Connell, recently arrived as the sole trade representative for an Irish company seeking to build an export-import business. O'Connell is well dressed and formal. When he presented his application it was impeccable. However, he showed no signs of offering a financial accommodation. Perhaps, Mohammed thought, this was just an oversight. Perhaps Mr. O'Connell did not realize how much authority Mohammed had in this situation. He told him that there was some further paperwork to be done and that he should come back in a few days.

O'Connell has been back twice. On each occasion he has become more irritated at the delays, but despite some broad hints dropped by Mohammed, he still has not offered any cash. So, Mohammed persisted in his approach: if Mr. O'Connell will not play the game according to the established rules, he will have to accept the consequences.

Back at his office, John O'Connell calls an old friend in Ireland, a man with experience in the country in question. The friend immediately realizes what the problem is and advises John how much he should offer and how he should make the offer. John becomes angry.

"But that's bribery!" he exclaims, "Pure corruption."

"No, it's just the way these people do things," says the friend. "Think of it as a tip."

In this example both Mohammed and John O'Connell are doing things the way they normally would in their own culture. This example shows that the cultural differences described in Chapter 2 are not just abstractions. They become part and parcel of the behavior of people from all cultures. In our day-to-day behavior we unconsciously act according to cultural norms—patterns of behavior specific to a particular culture. Scots the world round recognize the meaning and symbolic value of the words "Will ye have a wee dram?"—a drink, usually Scotch whisky, shared by the host with the guest at the beginning of a social visit. All cultures have such cues, such phrases, and such rituals.

In this chapter we look at how our cultural background and norms help us but also hinder us in our dealings with others, particularly culturally different others, by providing a kind of "cultural cruise control" that we rely on to guide our actions.

We show how it is often necessary to break out of our cultural cruise control by practicing *mindfulness,* a kind of thoughtful attention to cues provided by other people, situations, and cultures, and as a result to develop new *behavioral skills* of cross-cultural interaction. The combination of knowledge (Chapter 2), mindfulness, and behavioral skills is the basis of cultural intelligence. Throughout this chapter we return to the case of John and Mohammed to apply the components of cultural intelligence.

Cultural Scripts

A good way of thinking about the patterns of behavior described above is through the use of the term "script."[1] "Will ye have a wee dram?" is a line from a script. In the theater, a script tells the actor what he or she is supposed to say and sometimes gives guidance about how it should be said. In cultural rituals such as initiation ceremonies the script is often precise. But other scripts allow more scope for individual interpretation. There are scripts for Americans and scripts for Chinese, for instance, but they have some allowance for individual variation. For example, it may be possible within the workplace script of an American to be playfully disrespectful to a superior, but it would never be so for a Chinese.

Norms and scripts help us by telling us what to do. They prescribe patterns of behavior that feel comfortable for us because we observe them being practiced by members of the ingroup to which we belong or aspire to belong. The real problems occur when the norms and scripts of one culture clash with those of another, because, in order to interact, we must not only act out our own scripts, but also observe and make sense of others' actions based on *their* scripts. To do this we have to break out of our scripted behavior and switch off what we call cultural cruise control. Cultural cruise control means running your life on the basis of the inbuilt cultural assumptions that you derive from your own experience and culture—

your scripts. We call it cruise control because people let it happen automatically, without thinking about it. But it can be damaging because of the way it causes them to ignore other cultural signals.

In the case that opened this chapter, the Irishman O'Connell is operating on cultural cruise control with regard to Western conventions about financial inducements. He is unable to move outside the standard assumptions that prescribe behavior in his home culture. Even when his friend shows him the possibility of temporarily adopting a new set of principles, he discards it without consideration, slipping back to his own familiar framework. The bureaucrat Mohammed, too, shows signs of cultural cruise control. He assumes that John O'Connell is trying to take advantage of him, and thus fails to understand the genuine difficulty the Irishman faces. If either John or Mohammed had exercised the principles we describe in this chapter for getting out of cultural cruise control mode, they might have solved the problem. If *both* had done so, it might have been dealt with in only a few minutes.

Mindlessness

If you want to develop cultural intelligence you need to be able to suspend cultural cruise control and develop an alternative state of being called mindfulness.[2] A good starting point to understanding mindfulness is to examine its alternative—mindlessness—in the everyday activity of driving an automobile.

DRIVING

Mary, from Madison, Wisconsin, was born and brought up and lived for many years in the United States, where it is customary to drive a car with the controls on the left-hand side of the car and compulsory to drive on the right-hand side of the road. But on a visit to Europe, Mary met Eleanor, who was from Adelaide, Australia, and the two became close friends. In Australia—as in the United Kingdom, Japan, and some other countries—it is customary to drive a car with the controls on the right-hand side of the car and compulsory to drive on the left-hand side of the road. The roads are engineered and signposted accordingly. Both Mary and Eleanor were competent drivers, with licenses entitling them to drive anywhere in the world.

In her early forties, Mary went to live for a few years in the UK, where she had to drive right-hand drive cars on the left-hand side of the road. In *her* mid-forties, Eleanor went to live for a year in Germany, where she had to drive *left*-hand drive cars on the *right*-hand side of the road.

Both have vivid memories of their experiences. In the car with right-hand drive that Mary drove in England, the controls were also reversed. For example, the levers for the turn signal and the windscreen wipers were on the opposite side of the steering column from what she was used to. It was many months before Mary could consistently signal her intentions to turn instead of turning on her windscreen wipers. English drivers are used to proper signaling of turns and are very unforgiving of those who don't do it properly. The cacophony of horns hooting helped to remind Mary that turning on one's wipers was not an appropriate signal! In Germany, Eleanor had a minor collision with another car when turning left at a traffic light: she wasn't paying attention—in Australia turning left does not involve crossing the path of oncoming traffic. On another occasion she turned a corner on the wrong side of the road—fortunately there was no oncoming traffic—while her German passenger shouted, "Get over! Get over!"

Driving—and in particular driving on the correct side of the road—is a good example of mindlessness. Living is complex, but through superior learning abilities we humans have learned to simplify it by developing sequences of complex actions that we perform competently without paying conscious attention. When driving, we can steer, avoid obstacles, operate direction indicators, and brake when appropriate almost unconsciously. While we drive we can simultaneously listen to the news on the radio, reflect on the day's work, plan the evening meal, or even carry on a telephone conversation. When we follow familiar routes, we can even forget about navigating the car. Have you ever had the experience of arriving at your workplace or your home in your car after following a familiar route and noting with surprise, "I'm here! How did I get here? I guess I was thinking about something else!"

Mindlessness is not necessarily negative—in driving it simply means we drive without our minds fully engaged on the job. If we can do so safely, why not? Mindlessness has its advantages. It makes it possible for us to do more than one thing at a time. It enables us to ignore much of what goes on around us or to fit it automatically into an existing framework. In business situations, we can get on with business without having to worry about background factors such as culture.

However, the benefits of mindlessness are short-term and may be illusory. Mindlessness encourages us to rely on routine, and prevents us from being flexible in changing circumstances. Managers with "marketing myopia" blinker themselves with assumptions about the nature of their product. Managers who have been successful in the past mindlessly continue with the same approaches and techniques that brought them success and fail to notice that circumstances have changed. International managers from developed countries mindlessly assume that their role is to enlighten their counterparts in transition economies on "correct" actions in a market economy, even though such actions may be totally inappropriate for the different situation. These are all examples of trying to let cruise control do the work in changing conditions for which it was not designed.

Source of Cultural Scripts

Just as we have automatic cruise control when driving a car, we often operate on cruise control regarding culture. From an early age, we carry elements of our culture around with us.

Much learning is imitative. Children imitate the attitudes and behavior of their parents and other role models.[3] They become aware of ideas and ways of acting that are considered normal within the confines of their own culture. There are also the deliberate practices of socialization—learning programs at home, in school, in peer groups, and so forth—where rules of action, often derived from the culture or subculture, are deliberately passed on to newcomers.

For most of us, cultural cruise control makes our own culture the center of our mental universe and causes us to regard all others as deviant. Scripts from other cultures are not considered, and, if practiced by others, are likely to be unnoticed, ignored, or misunderstood. Even if what you learn is simply unease in the presence of those from other cultures, or a feeling that they are odd, this discomfort is likely to be built into your cruise control.

Cultural cruise control tends to work just fine as long as we are with people with whom we share underlying cultural assumptions and scripts—most likely people from the same background and social class, as well as culture. The cultural differences we indicated in Chapter 2 build in powerful assumptions too, almost like little voices urging others to Be Like Me! As long as others share the same cultural grounding, we can take culture for granted and focus on other matters such as making a deal. But when we are interacting with people whose cultural background is different, errors and misunderstandings quickly emerge, and the making of the deal is undermined.

We have all been in situations where someone has, to use an expression beloved by the English, "dropped a clanger" (that is, unwittingly said or done something offensive to the religion, ethnicity, background, or beliefs of someone else present). An example is putting out your hand to shake that of an orthodox Jew, not realizing that this familiarity is prohibited by his customs. Most clangers are caused by one person's continuing to make the assumptions of his or own culture without noticing that the other person has his or her own background and customs and should be treated differently.

How Culture Affects Behavior

Cultural programming also acts as a mental template against which new information from "out there"—the environment—is interpreted. We are not cameras: we do not take in neutral information from out there and reproduce it exactly on the film of our minds. We perceive information with cultural and other cues embedded in it and interpret it in light of our own preconceived frameworks. In the process differences and distortions occur.[4]

SELECTIVE PERCEPTION

At any given time, we can attend to only a fraction of the myriad of ever-changing stimuli the world presents us. When in cruise-control mode, we rely on our mental programming and screen out all that is not immediately and directly relevant. For example, in an emergency situation when driving we perceive information relevant to the emergency—for example, the road, other traffic, the sound of the car engine—and do not notice the expressions on the faces of passersby, the color of the upholstery in the car, or the music still playing on the car radio.

Cultural conditioning teaches us what to perceive and what to ignore. That is, people from different cultures can be presented with exactly the same situation and perceive it differently.

Suppose you are eating with someone at a restaurant, and he or she is talking about a business deal. If you are interested in business you will pay close attention to the words. But if you are, for example, a fashion expert or a chef, you may be more interested in what your companion is wearing or eating, and if you are romantically interested you may attend to what they look, sound, and smell like. If you are from a collectivist society you may look for information about their relationship with family or group, and if from an individualist society for evidence of their personal attainments. Your culture is one of the key factors that focuses your attention.

SOCIAL CATEGORIZATION

Another key mental process that helps us deal with all the information presented to us by the environment is called categorization. In social situations, this involves sorting other people (and ourselves) into different categories. This process is much like the way mail is sorted into pigeonholes. Each hole might be labeled with the last few digits of a postal code. As letters are sorted, the post office worker does not read the name or address on the letter but glances only at the postal code in order to put the letter in the proper bin. In this way the amount of information that must be dealt with by the sorter is greatly reduced. In order to be similarly efficient, we categorize people based on limited information.

Often we categorize others on the basis of appearance; in other cases we must attend to additional cues. Speech—language, accent, vocabulary, content—is an important source of cues. We tend to make in-group and out-group categorizations (see Chapter 2); that is, we classify people according to whether they belong, or do not belong, to groups of which we ourselves are members.

Other key indicators enable us to sort people into categories. For example:

- Race and gender are common indicators of belonging to a specific group.
- The extent to which a person stands out as different from others is another primary factor. For example, Europeans are obvious in rural Japan.
- People who are "typical" of their group are easier to categorize.

- A history of interaction with a group (particularly a history of conflict) makes it easier to categorize its members as not in our group.

Once we form a category, we perceive its members to be similar to each other. In contrast, we continue to see differences between members of our own groups. For example, an Asian person may be broadly aware of a category of "European," whereas a European may see many different categories within "European"—for example, Anglo Saxon, Celtic, Mediterranean, Scandinavian, and Slav—not to mention different national and regional categories.

STEREOTYPING

Categorizing people influences our attitudes about and expectations of them.[5] We tend to perceive everyone in the group as having particular characteristics and similar behaviors. We may expect Americans to be noisy, Irish gregarious, and Japanese polite. These stereotypes need not be negative but often are. When stereotypes contain negative attitudes and expectations they often lead to negative behavior or prejudice. Perhaps the most noxious prejudice toward others who are "not like me" is racism, in part because it is so easy to categorize others based on race.[6] Stereotypes of other nationalities may be intense, particularly when the group in question is salient in one's experience. Much political conflict—for instance, Arab-Israeli, Indian-Pakistani, Serbian-Kosovan, Irish Catholic–Irish Protestant—creates and is supported by intense negative stereotypes of respective out-groups. Stereotypes may be based on limited information or on the stereotypes of influential others. People can hold intense stereotypes of another culture without ever having met anyone from that culture. Furthermore, stereotypes perpetuate themselves, because through selective perception (see above), we tend to notice events and behavior that confirm our stereotypes and fail to notice information that disconfirms them.

In attribution we move beyond simple observation and interpretation of others to make inferences about *why* people might behave as they do. Particularly important is the distinction between internal attributions, in which behavior is attributed to factors associated with the person—for example, "she slapped her son because she is an aggressive person"—and external attributions, in which we believe behavior is caused by external circumstance—"she slapped her son because he misbehaved."

When categorization and the associated stereotypical expectations are combined with attribution, we get some interesting effects. For example, "she slapped her son because she is Serbian, and Serbians are well known to be cruel and aggressive people."

A common error is to attribute the behavior of members of an out-group to the same causes that would likely be true if members of our own in-group behaved the same way, as shown in the case below.

THE BOYFRIEND WHO WASN'T

A young American man devoted a lot of attention to a Japanese woman visiting his community, including extreme courtesy—taking her arm to cross the street, and so on. The young woman later told her friends excitedly that she now had an American boyfriend. In fact, the American, who was from the Deep South of the United States where many families pride themselves on effusive courtesy, was not interested in the Japanese girl as a prospective girlfriend. He had merely tried to be polite, in a manner that came naturally to him in his own in-group. Unfortunately, the same type of behavior practiced by a member of the Japanese woman's in-group would definitely have been evidence of a romantic interest.[7]

In the above case, both parties were operating in cultural cruise control. The American man continued to act automatically in the script of his own culture, without noticing the impression his behavior was making on his companion. The Japanese woman continued to observe automatically through the lens of her own culture and made no allowances for the difference in background. Without either meaning to, the two colluded to create a major misunderstanding. What was needed was for one or both to *switch off their cultural cruise control* and adopt a state of mindfulness in which they both become aware of the cultural significance of their own and the other's behavior.

Switching Off Cultural Cruise Control

A pilot whose airplane is set on cruise control—automatic pilot—knows that he or she can rely on the expert programming built into the automatic system to keep the plane flying straight and level and on the correct course, as long as conditions stay normal. But once in a while a change in conditions— a sudden weather hazard, a mechanical failure, or even the need to land the plane—will trigger warning signs. The pilot will snap out of mindlessness, switch off the automatic pilot, and devote all of his or her attention and skill to the problem.

Mary and Eleanor would have been crazy to rely on their cruise control during their first experiences of driving on the "wrong" side of the road. In novel cross-cultural situations, it is *imperative* that you consciously switch off your cultural cruise control. However, doing so is just the first step. Suspending cultural mindlessness means that you are attending to cultural issues. It does not follow that you are attending to them in a productive way. To get maximum benefit requires a new set of active practices, which we call mindfulness.

Mindfulness

Mindfulness is the opposite of mindlessness. In contrast to the mindless driving of Mary and Eleanor in their home countries, a professional race car driver will operate his or her vehicle mindfully, focusing all attention on the task of driving. Mindfulness is such a common idea that most of us do not appreciate how powerful it can be. It is basically *paying attention* to context. It means discarding the rigid mental programming that constrains our ability to see the forest for the trees. It does not mean abandoning who you are but rather using attention to become aware of differences and to think differently. It includes the recognition that despite cultural differences there will also be many similarities between us and people from other groups and that the cultural differences that do exist do not matter all the time.

In cross-cultural interactions, mindfulness means simultaneously

- *being aware* of our own assumptions, ideas, and emotions, as well as the selective perception, attribution, and categorization that we and others adopt
- *noticing* what is apparent about the other person and tuning in to *their* assumptions, words, and behavior
- using *all of the senses* in perceiving situations, rather than just relying on, for example, hearing the words that the other person speaks
- viewing the situation from *several perspectives*, that is, with an open mind
- attending to the *context* to help interpret what is happening
- creating new *mental maps* of other people's personalities and cultural backgrounds to assist us in responding appropriately to them
- creating new *categories* and recategorizing others into a more sophisticated category system
- *seeking out* fresh information to confirm or disconfirm the mental maps
- using *empathy*—the ability to mentally put ourselves in the other person's shoes as a means of understanding the situ-

ation and their feelings toward it, from the perspective of their cultural background rather than ours.

Mindfulness is a mediating step that helps us to link knowledge to skillful practice. It gives us *readiness* to interact with people who are different. It gives us the background to communicate comfortably and accurately in ways that honor the backgrounds and identities of both parties.

In the case that opened this chapter John O'Connell might have saved himself a great deal of time and aggravation by simply being mindful. A mindful John O'Connell would have been aware that his initial perception of Mohammed and his lack of cooperation might have been based on O'Connell's own expectations and may not have been accurate. He would have asked himself whether his attributions for Mohammed's behavior were simply projections of his own cultural programming. He would have noticed his own irritation and asked himself, "Why am I feeling this way?" In evaluating the situation he would have paid attention to Mohammed's situation and the working conditions in the Middle Eastern country. And, when presented with new information about the possible reasons for Mohammed's behavior, he would have suspended evaluation, had empathy for Mohammed, and perhaps would have created new mental categories that classified Mohammed as a hard-working civil servant rather than a crook and the expected payment as a normal business transaction rather than a moral breach.[8]

Being mindful takes a lot of effort, especially at first. But over time being mindful can become a natural and normal way of being. We don't have to be mindful all the time. But mindfulness does assist being in control and leads to greater freedom of thought and action.

Behavioral Skills

Knowledge and mindfulness are key elements in cultural intelligence, but in themselves they are not enough. In practice, cultural intelligence is seen in, and judged by, *behavior.* Cultural intelligence is not just a mind game—you have to be able to *perform.*

For example, in the case with which we started this chapter, it is insufficient for Mohammed and John O'Connell to understand each other's culturally based attitudes to unofficial payments and to practice mindfulness in their picking up of cues from each other in their interactions. They also need to be able to interact with each other in a suitable way, so that each feels relaxed, confident, and able to work together to reach a good conclusion. The third and last element of cultural intelligence is *behavioral skills.*

Behavioral scientists have long been aware that the concept of skill can be applied to social behavior. The most commonly perceived causes of problems in businesses are not technical or administrative deficiencies but problems such as communication failures, misunderstandings in negotiations, personality conflicts, poor leadership style, and bad teamwork—in other words, inadequacies in the ways that people interact with each other.

Nowadays, many organizations regard social skills or interpersonal skills as key qualifications for new employees. Upward of 70 percent of most managers' time, in most cultures, is typically spent in interaction with others—superiors, subordinates, peers, clients, and others—in face-to-face conversations, meetings, telephone calls, and informal social settings. Skilled interpersonal performance is vital, and many companies offer skills training as part of their employee development programs.

Most of us have at one time or another admired the social performance of colleagues and others who are virtuosos in the art of interpersonal communication and relationship-building. Each of us also, to a greater or lesser degree, has his or her own set of skilled social behaviors, and these are closely related to expectations and scripts of our own culture. Some of the social skills we develop in our own cultures may contain elements—such as willingness to initiate a conversation, interest in other people, and listening skills—that may assist us in other cultural settings. However, operating in new cultures also creates a new frontier for our social interactions, probably requiring the development of quite new social performance.

Acquiring the skills of cultural intelligence is not about becoming more skilled in a particular behavior or set of behaviors but about extending the range, or *repertoire*,[9] of skilled behaviors and knowing when to use each one. Cultural difference extends the range of possibilities that you may face. Skilled routines you have mastered to a high level of performance in one culture may be counterproductive in another, to the extent that you have to "unlearn" them in the new situation. Here is a case in point.

FRENCH DRESSING

Philippe LeBeau was a stereotypically dark, handsome Frenchman. He was known particularly as a ladies' man who knew how to be charming to women and make them feel good about themselves. This was particularly important in the Paris media company where Philippe worked as a manager, because the majority of employees were women.

Philippe had noticed that many of the women in the company took pride in dressing fashionably and well. He therefore made a point of frequently complimenting them on their appearance—for example, "Marie, that is such a chic outfit! You look as beautiful today as I have ever seen you." This kind of comment almost always gained him a smile, a blush, a thank you, and more importantly, he felt, increased cooperation from the woman to whom he had paid the compliment.

One day it was announced that Phillippe's company had been taken over by a major international conglomerate based in the United States. When the dust of the merger had settled, Philippe was delighted to find he was to be transferred for a two-year assignment to the company headquarters in New Jersey. He was given a briefing on the U.S. and its different social norms and was advised, for example, that touching other people, particularly those of the opposite sex, was much less acceptable there than in France. He resolved therefore to be careful about his French habit of showing positive feelings to his French colleagues by occasionally taking their hands in his, kissing them on the cheek, and the like.

In New Jersey, his new secretary, Anita Courtenay, turned out to be a highly effective person as well as a strikingly beautiful one, who, like many of his French colleagues, dressed extremely well. Phillippe was careful to keep his physical distance from Anita as he had been taught, but he felt that her obvious glamour provided an opportunity to build a good relationship. So in his customary French manner he would greet her every morning with a freshly minted compliment on her appearance. Her initial reaction was surprise. After a few days she would thank him politely and then change the subject. Then she began to respond by frowning and pursing her lips. Philippe was puzzled. She really was an outstanding secretary as well as a beautiful woman. Did she think his compliments were insincere? And was it his imagination, or was she wearing less chic outfits with each passing day? Was she also using less makeup?

On the third morning of Philippe's second week at work, he arrived at work to find Anita seated at her desk, apparently wearing no makeup and with an outfit that was neat and tasteful but that did nothing to show off the beauty of its wearer. However, even in such modest attire, Anita looked fresh and lovely, and Philippe said so: "Anita, once more you are looking wonderful. Seeing your beauty makes my heart beat faster, and I know that I will work better today because of it."

She looked at him with astonishment and then slowly got to her feet. "Mr. LeBeau," she said levelly, "I want you to stop making comments on my personal appearance. I am not here as a decoration, I am here as an employee. I take a real pride in what I do, but all you can talk about is the way I look. Can you imagine how that makes me feel? I have tried to discourage you, but it seems you won't take a hint. And if you have any ideas about getting involved with me, you can forget them—I have a boyfriend and I don't want another. So from now on, can you please treat me with a bit more respect and professionalism?"

In this case, Philippe develops a repertoire of skilled behavior that works well in one cultural situation but breaks down in another. His performance is based on a particular "French" view of the world, on ways of expressing himself most likely developed from childhood, on sheer habit, and on having previously had the habit consistently rewarded. It will be hard for Philippe LeBeau, socially skilled as he is, to erase the habits that don't work in his new environment and to replace them with new, appropriate forms of social performance. First he will need to gain a better understanding of the history and norms of male-female interaction in his new culture (knowledge). Then he will have to pay more attention to the behavioral cues provided by Anita and the other women with whom he interacts (mindfulness). Lastly he will need to develop new ways of behaving towards women; he will have to experiment with and refine them (behavioral skills).

The specific behavioral skills that are required by managers operating across cultures span the gamut of interactions and interpersonal relationships in organizations. In our opening case study, John O'Connell and Mohammed need *interpersonal skills* in order to conduct the conversations needed to resolve the current problem. They may need *negotiation skills* to determine an appropriate level of payment by John and service by Mohammed. If they wish to move beyond the present transaction and to build a good relationship for the future, they will need *relationship-building skills*.

However, John's relationship with Mohammed—that of expatriate client to local bureaucrat—may not be the only one he has to cultivate in his new job. He may also have to relate to local organizations, take part in local social events, and employ local staff. These additional situations and considerations increase the range of required skills: for example, *etiquette skills* (such as those in which Philippe LeBeau was so conspicuously lacking in his American cultural setting) enabling appropriate performance in formal ceremonies, rituals, and social events; *influencing skills* and *selling skills* in promoting his company's business; and *leadership skills* and *teamwork skills* enabling John to put together a local organization and manage local staff. There may even be special skills such as those necessary for telephone conversation, report writing, and decision making, where there are subtle differences between John's habitual Irish style and the expectations of his new setting, where he again has to develop or refine what he does.

Skilled Performance

One way of understanding the skills aspect of cultural intelligence is to think of yourself as a *performer*. The notion of skilled performance has been applied to many different areas of human endeavor. Diana Krall singing a jazz standard or Tiger Woods hitting a perfect drive epitomizes the smooth and apparently effortless production of behaviors that exercise near-perfect control over parts of the physical world. These virtuoso performers have enormous physical and mental talent in their chosen fields, yet each has also spent many years of hard work perfecting her or his art.

A key element in cultural intelligence is *adaptability*. Whether or not social behavior takes place in a cross-cultural setting, each situation will be unique and in particular will involve interaction with other unique people. As a skilled social performer, you will have to be able instantaneously to adapt your general approach and specific interactions to the particular characteristics of the situation and, particularly, to the expectations of the other people involved. Cross-cultural skills are not fixed routines but flexible abilities that can—with the guidance of mindfulness—be modified to meet new or changing conditions. Even within a given culture you will find that people vary in the extent to which they conform to underlying cultural norms. The culturally intelligent person's social performance draws on a repertoire of potential behaviors. With the assistance of mindfulness, the performer is able constantly to monitor the environment and to select, deploy, and modify appropriate routines from this wide resource.

Summary

This chapter describes the ways in which our cultural programming affects our behavior and our interactions with others who are culturally different. Much of the time, we operate on a kind of cultural cruise control in which our mental programming directs our behavior without much conscious thought. This programming allows us to go about our daily routine without actively thinking about every little thing we do. However, in cross-cultural interactions this mindless behavior can cause problems. Through selective perception, stereotypical expectations, and inaccurate attributions, our own cultural programming may lead us to misjudge the behavior of others who are culturally different. To counteract the tendency to function on cultural cruise control we advocate practicing mindfulness, an active awareness that is a critical link between knowledge about culture and appropriate behavior in cross-cultural situations. The mindful individual also needs to increase his or her repertoire of skilled behaviors, particularly social behaviors and to be able to deploy these appropriately in different cultural settings. The elements of knowledge, mindfulness, and skills enable the practice of cultural intelligence in skilled performance adapted to the special cultural setting that the individual faces.

CHAPTER 4

Raising Your Cultural Intelligence

THE BULL IN THE CHINA SHOP

Shortly after Barbara Bull began her first overseas assignment at her United States–based company's hotel in Beijing, she discovered differences in managerial culture. At the time she was public relations manager for the hotel. Here's what happened.

Barbara had assigned Weixing Li, one of her staff members, to take photographs of a VIP arriving and being greeted by the management team. However, five minutes before the appointed time, Weixing Li was nowhere to be found. Barbara ended up taking the photographs herself. The staff member eventually showed up late, about five minutes after the VIP guest's arrival.

Barbara initially reacted with anger and frustration. But she restrained herself. When they got back to the office, she took Weixing Li aside. She thought that given the circumstances he seemed much too nonchalant. So she asked,

"Do you know what you did wrong?"

His response was a blank stare.

Again she said, "Do you know what you did wrong? Do you know why I am upset?"

Another blank look.

"Don't you even know what you have done wrong?" she said.

" Whatever you say I did wrong, I did wrong," he replied.

Barbara was taken aback. Was he being a smart aleck? "I want you to tell me what you did wrong!" she said.

"Whatever you say I did wrong, I did wrong. You are the boss. I'm sure whatever you say is correct. So whatever you say I did wrong, I will admit to."

This response made her even angrier. So she proceeded to tell him exactly what he had done wrong, describing his irresponsible actions, immaturity, and failure. He apologized and said no more. He looked downcast, but Barbara was not sure that he understood the problem or that he would change his behavior.

The fact that this encounter didn't turn out the way she had expected caused her to ask her fellow manager Chrissie about the problem. Chrissie had been in China for several years. When Barbara described what had happened, Chrissie nodded.

"It's a common problem," she said. "And in order to get it right you need to understand how important *mianzi is* to Chinese people."

"*Mianzi?* What's that?"

"We would call it 'face,' as in 'saving face' or 'losing face.' *Mianzi* is the motivating force behind a lot of actions in Chinese culture."

Chrissie explained that the problem was that Chinese employees such as Weixing Li saw things from a hierarchical viewpoint. It's likely he recognized that he had done something wrong, but his way of handling it would have been to let his boss, who was at the top of the hierarchy, point out what he should have done differently. In the action that she took, Barbara had made him lose face, which was bad for the long-term relationship and for his commitment to the hotel. It was good that Barbara had not reprimanded him in front of others, but it would be ludicrous to think that no one else knew about this situation.

Barbara, said Chrissie, should not have criticized Weixing Li for his actions, or caused him to lose face in front of his colleagues. But in Weixing Li's eyes the concept of face would apply not just to him but to Barbara. What she should have done was to highlight how his actions had caused *her* (and thus the hotel) to lose face, causing him shame. Chrissie was certain from her own experience that this method of handling the situation would have got the results Barbara wanted.

Barbara made a mental note to remember Chrissie's advice the next time she felt like blowing her top. At the same time, she thought, being in a foreign country is like walking on eggshells. People's egos are so easily crushed. She wondered, How am I supposed to know these things? How do I learn to get it right? How can I practice?

In the situation above Barbara improved her cultural intelligence through experiential learning. She was able to build on the failed interaction to gain knowledge from her colleague. Her newfound understanding should enable her to become more mindful and to develop a new set of skills that she can apply to other cross-cultural interactions. In short, she became more culturally intelligent.

Cultural Intelligence

Let's recap the concept of cultural intelligence. In its broadest sense cultural intelligence is the capability to interact effectively with people from different cultural backgrounds. Like other forms of intelligence such as social intelligence (the capability of interacting with others), and emotional intelligence (the capability of regulating and using one's emotional states), cultural intelligence is composed of many facets. Cultural intelligence enables us to recognize cultural differences through knowledge and mindfulness and gives us a propensity and ability to act appropriately across cultures. The culturally intelligent manager draws on a breadth of experience and can make fine discriminations among subtly different behaviors that perfectly fit the situation. One manager called this ability "a matrix in the minds of managers."[1]

Cultural intelligence explains why some intelligent people with good social skills and characteristics associated with high emotional maturity can still have problems adjusting properly to a new cultural context. They may be smart and socially adept, but they lack a high CQ, as the following example demonstrates.

HR TRAINING IN HANOI

Don Buck stormed into the Hanoi office of the international consultancy for which he worked. A Canadian training specialist, he had been sent to Vietnam to train the owners of small and medium-sized businesses in human resource management practices using market-oriented approaches rather than the socialist seniority-based system they were used to. He had been transferred to the Vietnam assignment because of his prior effectiveness over ten years of working on similar issues with Russian managers.

However, over the months he had worked in Vietnam the cross-cultural adjustment problems had begun to mount. Don's current complaint to his manager, Stephanie Reichman, was, "I've taught this course many times—in Russia, in the Ukraine, and in Canada and the U.S. It's always worked before. But here . . . they want answers; they want me to tell them the right answer when there isn't one. They want structure; they want to know exactly what I think, they want to write it down and memorize it. They want to learn facts but they don't want to learn to *think!* I want to encourage discussion and thinking, and they don't see that. Don't they realize they would learn much more if they would just do it my way?"

Stephanie sighed. To her, Don was just another in a long line of trainers who were in difficulty because they hadn't been flexible enough to adapt their methods to the new situation. When Don had arrived in Hanoi she had tried to explain the differences, but Don had been so self-confident because of his success in Russia that she now doubted if he had noticed.[2]

Don's complaint centers on *learning styles*. In Canada and Russia he had got used to a particular style of learning. He and his North American and Russian students shared a belief in what is called the constructivist method of education and training, in which the teacher, rather than being a powerful authority figure who knows the "right answer," helps students to build their knowledge and skills in their own ways and to come to their own conclusions. It seems that the cultural framework he had learned in Canada transferred itself to the United States and Russia without too many problems. But Vietnam was different. Vietnam is a high "power distance" culture (see Chapter 2), which means that students tend to defer to the authority figure (the trainer) and expect him or her to know all the answers. Also, historical relationships between the Vietnamese and a series of colonial powers have influenced people's attitudes toward those in authority. Frustrated by this situation, Don's response, as we discussed in Chapter 3, was to resort to cruise control and his well-worn behavioral script.

Don is one of the many overseas managers who are not born with high cultural intelligence. Cultural intelligence develops (is learned) over time; however, as shown in the above example, experience in foreign cultures does not mean that someone will automatically develop high cultural intelligence. Individuals must have the capacity to develop cultural intelligence and be motivated to do so as well.

Knowing what cultural intelligence is does not on its own enable any manager to acquire it. Barbara Bull and Don Buck in the cases above are just two among the many overseas managers who find that not only are they lacking in cultural intelligence, but they do not know how to acquire it. Is it something we are born with? Is it something we learn? If we learn it, can we learn it comfortably, ahead of time, in familiar surroundings, or do we have to head overseas and learn it by experience in other countries? And whose responsibility is it to create the learning opportunities—the individual's or that of the company that sends the individual overseas?

Characteristics Supportive of Cultural Intelligence

Individuals can learn to be more culturally intelligent. However, some characteristics that individuals already possess or can develop make them more motivated and more able to increase their cultural intelligence. These are integrity, openness, and hardiness.[3]

INTEGRITY

Here integrity means having a well-developed sense of self and understanding how one's own belief system motivates behavior. Understanding oneself is a fundamental base for cultural intelligence. Each of us has a sense of ourselves as physically unique. However, we differ in the ways we describe our inner self—the thoughts and feelings that cannot be directly known by other people. For some of us this means being autonomous and unique, and for others it means being connected to others. We can also see ourselves as essentially equal to everyone else or as naturally superior or subordinate. How we think of ourselves influences the way we behave and the way we interact with others. It is important for us to have an *honest* understanding of ourselves. In this way, integrity also implies completeness and well roundedness. Individuals with high integrity are not threatened by views or behavior that is very different from their own.

OPENNESS (HUMILITY AND INQUISITIVENESS)

Humility means showing deferential respect and a willingness to learn from others. It is passive openness or open-mindedness. People with high openness are not necessarily timid or unassuming but are conscious that their own views are fallible. Another type of openness is active openness or inquisitiveness. This is curiosity—the inclination to investigate and pursue knowledge. In this case we mean inquisitiveness particularly about people from other cultures. Without inquisitiveness, opportunities to develop cultural intelligence through interacting with others are often declined or wasted.

HARDINESS

Hardiness is robustness, courage, intrepidness, and capability of surviving unfavorable conditions. If we are hardy we can cope with stress, recover from shocks, and perceive stressful events as interesting and meaningful and as an opportunity for growth and learning. Interacting with people from other cultures, whether at home or in a foreign country, involves ambiguity, tension, and emotion. Developing hardiness is valuable as we go through the repeated interactions required to become culturally intelligent.

While everyone can become more culturally intelligent, the possession or development of these underlying characteristics—integrity, openness, and hardiness—can support and make your acquisition of a cultural intelligence easier. These traits improve your capacity for acquiring the behavioral repertoire needed in order for you to be culturally intelligent. Again, mindfulness is key. Being mindful of your sense of self, of what is driving you to behave as you do is fundamental. This awareness, combined with the active pursuit of openness and hardiness, lays a foundation for developing a high level of cultural intelligence.

Developmental Stages of CQ

The development of cultural intelligence occurs in several stages.

- *Stage 1: Reactivity to external stimuli.* A starting point is a mindless adherence to one's own cultural rules and norms. This stage is typical of individuals with very little exposure to, or interest in, other cultures. Parochial individuals do not even recognize that cultural differences exist. If they do, they consider them inconsequential. People at this stage of development can be heard to say things like "I don't see differences. I treat everyone the same."

- *Stage 2: Recognition of other cultural norms and motivation to learn more about them.* Experience and mindfulness produce a newfound awareness of the multicultural mosaic that surrounds us. A heightened sense of mindfulness presents a sometimes-overwhelming amount of new information. Curiosity is aroused and the individual wants to learn more. People at this stage often struggle to sort through the complexity of the cultural environment. They search for simple rules of thumb to guide their behavior.

- *Stage 3: Accommodation of other cultural norms and rules in one's own mind.* Reliance on absolutes disappears. A deeper understanding of cultural variation begins to develop. The cultural norms and rules of various societies begin to seem comprehensible and even reasonable in their context. The recognition of appropriate behavioral responses to different cultural situations develops, but adaptive behavior takes a lot of effort and is often awkward. People at this stage know what to say and do in a variety of cultural situations. However, they have to think about what they are doing, and adaptive behavior does not feel natural.

- *Stage 4: Assimilation of diverse cultural norms into alternative behaviors.* At this stage, adjusting to different situations no longer requires much effort. Individuals develop a repertoire of behaviors from which they can choose depending on the specific cultural situation. They function in a number of different cultures almost effortlessly and with no more stress than if they were in their home culture. Members of other cultures accept them as culturally knowledgeable and feel comfortable interacting with them. They feel at home almost anywhere.

- *Stage 5: Proactivity in cultural behavior based on recognition of changing cues that others do not perceive.* Highly culturally intelligent people have the ability to sense changes in cultural context, sometimes even before members of the other culture. They are so attuned to the nuances of intercultural interactions that they automatically adjust their behavior to anticipate these changes and facilitate better intercultural interactions among others. They intuitively know what behaviors are required and how to execute them effectively. Individuals at this stage of development may be quite rare, but they demonstrate a level of cultural intelligence to which we all might aspire.

People at higher levels of cultural intelligence have a *cognitively complex* perception of their environment. They are able to make connections between seemingly disparate pieces of information. They describe people and events in terms of many different characteristics and are able to see the many links among these characteristics. They can see a coherent pattern in a cultural situation without knowing what the final picture might look like.

Culturally intelligent individuals are able to see past the stereotypes that a superficial understanding of cultural dimensions—such as collectivism, uncertainty avoidance, and power distance (see Chapter 2)—provide. These dimensions are only a first step (part of the knowledge component) of developing cultural intelligence.[4] Culturally intelligent people see the connections between a culture and its context, history, and value orientations. They realize that knowledge of the culture of a country or region is only valuable in the context of understanding its religious, philosophical, and historical issues. For example the Kurds, Shia Muslims, and Sunni Muslims in Iraq share many aspects of their cultural background. But an understanding of the history of their interactions over the centuries is necessary for a truly accurate understanding of the values, attitudes, and beliefs that underlie their behavior toward each other and the outside world.

The Process of Developing Cultural Intelligence

As outlined in Chapter 1, cultural intelligence involves the three components of knowledge, mindfulness, and skills. Raising your CQ is not a linear process but requires experiential learning that can take considerable time. It requires a base

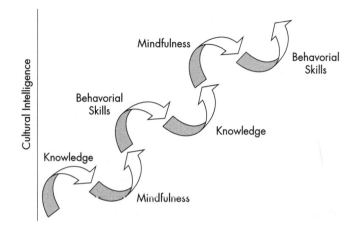

FIGURE 4.1. Gaining cultural intelligence

level of knowledge, the acquisition of new knowledge and alternative perspectives through mindfulness, and the accommodation and assimilation of this knowledge into behavioral skills. The process is iterative and can be thought of as a series of S curves as shown in Figure 4.1.[5]

The acquisition of cultural intelligence involves learning from social interactions. We have known for a long time that such social learning[6] is a very powerful way in which people's experiences are transferred into knowledge and skills. Social learning involves *attention* to the situation, *retention* of the knowledge gained from the situation, *reproduction* of the behavioral skills observed, and finally *reinforcement* (receiving feedback) about the effectiveness of the adapted behavior.

Improving CQ by learning from social experience means paying attention to, and appreciating, critical differences between oneself and others in culture and background. This, of course, requires some knowledge about the ways in which cultures differ, and how culture affects behavior. It also implies mindfulness of the context of the interaction and an openness to the legitimacy and importance of different behavior. Retaining this knowledge also requires the ability to transfer knowledge gained from a specific experience to broader skills that can be used in future interactions and in other settings. Reproduction means practicing the skills learned in future interactions; and, finally, reinforcement implies that the more frequently and mindfully behaviors are tried out and are successful, the more quickly cultural intelligence improves.

As implied by the diagram in Figure 4.1, improving your CQ takes time, and you must be motivated to do it. The iterative and long-term nature of gaining cultural intelligence is illustrated in the following example.

> UNDERSTANDING THE FRENCH
>
> Jenny Stephens is a thirty-five-year-old executive working for the French subsidiary of an American multinational. After meeting and marrying a Frenchman in New York she moved to Paris, where she has lived for seven years. She speaks fluent French and interacts with French relatives and friends and colleagues on a regular basis. When asked if she felt she understood French culture she said, "I have been here for seven years. In an almost predictable manner, I have found that whenever I would begin to get a sense that I really understand the French, something strange would happen that will throw me off completely. As I would reflect on the event and talk it over with my husband and friends, I would begin to develop a more complex view of the French. Then, things would go fine for several months until the whole process would repeat itself in some other area."[7]

In this case Jenny is practicing a kind of mindfulness by recognizing unusual things that she observes as being related to culture and talking them over with her husband and friends. In this way, each instance of strange French behavior builds on her previous knowledge and contributes to her development of cultural intelligence.

Activities That Support the Development of Cultural Intelligence

Perhaps the most important means of increasing cultural intelligence is spending time overseas, thereby gaining international experience during which cross-cultural experiences will be frequent, and CQ will increase through necessity. Favorite strategies of Americans, according to one study,[8] are:

- Working for an international company
- Studying abroad
- Moving to a country of choice and actively seeking employment
- International tourism
- International internship
- Finding an international business mentor
- Teaching English abroad
- Government foreign service
- Multicultural team assignment, including "virtual" teams with members in different countries
- Foreign mission/humanitarian service
- Foreign military service

While overseas experiences are ideal, there are numerous situations and activities you can draw upon to increase cultural intelligence. These range from formal education to various informal interactions. For many people the motivation to become more culturally intelligent comes from developing a close relationship with someone who is culturally different.

Each of the activities outlined below can be important for developing cultural intelligence.

The types of formal training available to help you improve your CQ can be classified according to the extent that they are experiential (as opposed to purely factual) and the extent to which they are culture-specific or applicable across cultures. All of these types of training are valuable, but, as we suggested in Chapter 1, true cultural intelligence requires learning from experience, and building knowledge that develops skills that can then be applied across cultures. The following chart shows the types of formal training available and how they apply to our model of developing a high CQ.

TRAINING METHOD	APPLICATION TO CQ
Factual Books, lectures, area briefings	Knowledge about specific cultures, culture dimensions, and processes
Analytical Films, culture assimilators, sensitivity training	Both culture-general and culture-specific knowledge as well as the opportunity to practice mindfulness
Experiential Simulations, field trips, role-playing	Opportunities to practice both mindfulness and behavior skills, and to experience the emotions of cross-cultural interaction

Of the three methods, experiential training is the most rigorous and effective in developing a high CQ. But formal experiential training is rare and often expensive. To become culturally intelligent, therefore, most of us rely on our day-to-day interactions with people who are culturally different. Several contexts in which these interactions occur are worth mentioning here. These are cross-cultural teams, overseas assignments, and interactions with culturally different individuals at home.

CROSS-CULTURAL GROUPS AND TEAMS

Increasingly, the world's work is performed by groups or work teams. Additionally, many people are involved in social and interest groups. Because of globalization, the groups we belong to are increasingly composed of people from different cultures. We consider the management of multicultural work groups or teams in detail in Chapter 8. However, it is important to note here that, in addition to being a management challenge, multicultural groups offer a rich opportunity to gain cultural intelligence without necessarily leaving your own country. Culturally diverse groups offer you the opportunity to observe the behavior of culturally different individuals in the same context. That is, you can observe how the various cultures in a group respond to the assignment of group roles, the establishment of a leader, the imposition of deadlines, and all the other activities and processes of working in a group. Also, if you are a mindful person you will be able to catalog the wide variety of reactions to their own group behavior from culturally different members. The interactions of culturally different people in group settings are complex, but that complexity generates great learning opportunities. Thus diversity within the groups you work in should be seen not as a threat, but as an opportunity for you to develop greater cultural intelligence by using role models.

OVERSEAS EXPERIENCE
AND EXPATRIATE ASSIGNMENTS

One of the most challenging situations in which you may be able to confront cultural differences is a temporary period of living and working in a foreign country. In Chapter 9 we look at overseas experience in detail in relation to careers and make the point that such experiences may be self-initiated or may be driven by your firm's needs. This situation too offers you opportunities for intense experiential learning. If, like most people, you have had very little cross-cultural training before going overseas, you will have to adjust "on the fly." The overseas experience, unlike that of working in teams, is typically focused on a single culture in which one is immersed. Because of this immersion the experience tends to be intense and emotionally charged. Working in a foreign culture will result in high stress levels until you adjust. As in any cross-cultural interaction, the background characteristics of integrity and openness are important, but it is the characteristic of hardiness that may determine the extent to which your time overseas will result in a higher CQ. When everything and everyone seems to be working against you, it is extremely difficult to see the situation as interesting and a meaningful learning experience.

BUT I AM CHINESE!

A Chinese American with a master's degree in international business, who spoke Chinese, had taken an overseas assignment in China working for a multinational food-processing firm. She felt she would be a bridge between the Chinese and American managers in the firm. However, she was surprised when she realized that she had misunderstood the work environment in China. A year into the assignment she had the following observation: "My understanding of managing effectively came primarily from trial and error. I learned the hard way, falling on my face. But each time I fell, I'd assess what the critical learning of each incident was. I think that one must have an open mind when accepting an overseas assignment. China has one of the highest expatriate assignment failure rates in the world. I believe that the lack of ability to manage across cultures is at the top of the list of reasons. And, the reason for this is that expatriates fail to understand the thought processes and motivation of local employees."[9]

This case demonstrates that cultural intelligence is often gained by trying out new behaviors and being mindful of their effect. Learning from each cross-cultural interaction, even if it doesn't always work out as planned, is an important way to improve cultural intelligence. Also, the observation of the protagonist that understanding the thought processes and motivation of local employees is important to expatriate success cannot be overemphasized. As we discuss in more detail in Chapter 9, overseas assignments, perhaps more than any situation, require trying to understand the behavior of others from their own rather than your own cultural background.

CROSS-CULTURAL INTERACTIONS AT HOME

Our multicultural society may present you with numerous opportunities to engage with others who are culturally different. However, these interactions are often superficial and lack the depth and intensity of interpersonal interaction that is required for you to enjoy experiential learning. In the same way that leadership skills are often taught in terms of challenging outdoor activities such as ropes courses, significant CQ development will probably require you to move outside your comfort zone. For a westerner, having dinner at a Cantonese restaurant and interacting with the service people is indeed an intercultural interaction, but it is a very mild experience (although it might become a bit more intense if you order chicken feet!) and lacks significant engagement. Those who seek to become more culturally intelligent need to challenge themselves in deeper ways than this type of experience allows.

In our international management courses we routinely require our students to engage in a nontrivial cross-cultural experience in their local area in order to practice the skills they have learned in class. "Culture" in this case is not confined to national or ethnic culture, but, consistent with our definition in this book, can be any social group, and subcultures in a society provide excellent learning experiences. We tell students that if they are to learn they should feel culturally uncomfortable in the situation, at least at first. Some ways to engage in cross-cultural experiences are:

- Attend a religious service or wedding ceremony of someone from another culture. Ask a member to explain the significance of the rituals involved.

- Locate an ethnic organization in your community and attend (participating if possible) a cultural celebration. Ask members to explain the significance of the event and the symbolism of activities.

- Find an interest group that represents a set of beliefs to which you do not subscribe and attend one of their meetings. For example, our heterosexual university students have attended meetings of gay and lesbian associations. One of our mature executive students attended "bass and drums night" at a nightclub with her son—a major excursion into a foreign "youth culture." The following is an excerpt from her report.

BASS AND DRUMS NIGHT AT THE LOTUS CLUB

For my cross-cultural experience, I went to "bass and drums night" at the Lotus Club on Abbott Street. The Lotus is one of Vancouver's underground rave-type clubs. Ordinarily, I really would not have known such clubs existed. And certainly I would never have considered actually going into one. But, as it happens, my son, who is a jazz musician, is visiting right now, and he offered (as a joke, I think) to take me. I leapt at the opportunity to find out something about his world as well as fulfill my course requirements. I lost some of my enthusiasm when I found out what time the event took place (beginning at 11:00 p.m.) and what it involved.

The Lotus Hotel . . . looks really old, beer stained, maybe opium stained, with a kind of elemental grime I associate with the New York subway covering every surface. . . .

There's a way people look when they sleep all day and get up at 7:00 or 8:00 p.m. and go out at night. They get a night-person look.

The sound was so intense that at first it was an effort to walk towards it, to actually penetrate the wall of cigarette smoke and noise. Once inside it was more like a bath of music, wave after wave, pulsating, the walls were moving, the room was moving, everything was moving. I could feel a sensation like a force rhythmically pressing my chest . . . I realized I was tensing every muscle as though resisting a blow and found if I relaxed into it, it became a lot easier, even sort of energizing.

The dancers were incredible—moves like you see on TV . . . The music didn't seem to have a beginning or end, either. It just went on and on. . . .

[Their] outfits had that air of being carefully chosen to represent something—I just didn't know what it was.

I felt very conspicuous. My main reaction was to get into a corner, almost to hide. I wanted to watch without being noticed.

I felt overwhelmed. After a while, those feelings went away and were replaced by a kind of sadness. . . .

I could have danced, I guess, but I would have looked ridiculous. At least I thought I would look ridiculous. I felt like a foreigner, someone who would not be welcome and would somehow interrupt the flow. . . . There was no way I belonged in that group.

As more people showed up, I began to feel nervous. Some people looked strange and menacing, with leather, tattoos, body piercing in places I found to be weird.

I felt like I needed a friend in this cold, loud, unfamiliar world. I caught a few glimpses of my son as he flitted from here to there, dancing, drinking beer, and talking to people. Finally, he said, "Let's go home."

I was really happy to see the outside world . . . I've done my fair share of traveling and even lived abroad for four years. [This experience] reminded me that there is a lot going on around me that I don't know about. And, I do think I experienced a little, tiny bit of what it's like to have to function in a distant culture, where nothing is as usual, and even things that seem familiar turn out to be strange.

The Lotus Club case is a good example of mindfulness in action and the development of cultural intelligence. The uncomfortable situation made it difficult for the student to operate on cultural cruise control, but the vivid description of the situation shows an acute attention to the behavior of the culturally different others and the situational context. Also, this case shows that cross-cultural interactions can be found in your own backyard as well as outside your country's borders.

Regardless of the specific context for interaction with other cultures, there are several "rules of engagement" that you should try to keep in mind as you approach interactions with others who are culturally different. These are:

- Become knowledgeable about your own culture and background, its biases and idiosyncrasies, and the way this is unconsciously reflected in your own perceptions and behavior.

- Deliberately avoid mindlessness by expecting differences in others. See different behavior as novel, and suspend evaluation of it.

- Switch into a mindfulness mode in which you are attentive to behavioral cues and their possible interpretations and the likely effect of your behavior on others.

- Adapt your behavior in ways that you are comfortable with and you believe are appropriate for the situation.

- Be mindful of responses to your behavioral adaptation.

- Experiment with methods of adapting intuitively to new situations, and use these experiments to build your comfort level in acquiring a repertoire of new behavior.

- Practice new behaviors that work until their production becomes automatic.

Summary

This chapter defines the concept of cultural intelligence as the capability to interact effectively with people from different cultural backgrounds. Developing the repertoire of behaviors needed to become culturally intelligent requires finding development experiences that involve both knowledge (of oneself and others) and the application of mindfulness. The development of cultural intelligence goes through a series of stages ranging from simply reacting to external stimuli to proactively adjusting behavior in anticipation of subtle changes in the cultural context. While cultural intelligence can be developed, there are some underlying characteristics of individuals that support its development. These are integrity, openness, and hardiness. Cultural intelligence can be developed in a number of ways, including through formal education and training. However, experiential learning is critical to the development of a high CQ. Our multicultural environment provides many opportunities for raising our CQ. By following a few simple guidelines you can improve your cultural intelligence and develop the ability to act competently across a wide range of cultures, adding an extremely valuable skill to your repertoire.

CHAPTER 5

Decision Making Across Cultures

DECISIVENESS OR CONSENSUS?

Fresci Corporation is an Italian distribution company, with subsidiaries in a number of developed countries around the world. One of the managers is Tom Hammond, who runs the Canadian operation from Toronto. Another is Hoshi Yamamoto, chief of the Japanese subsidiary based in Tokyo. Tom and Hoshi met some years ago in a Fresci executive development program in Turin and have been friends ever since.

Every six months Fresci runs a meeting for all its international CEOs, holding the meetings in a different country each time. The company CEO, Alessandro Bortolo, asks each national subsidiary to report its results for the previous half year, which can then be scrutinized by all the company's top executives. Reporting results is a bit of an ordeal, especially for those managers whose subsidiaries have fallen short of their expected performance. Fresci and Mr. Bortolo do not tolerate poor performance, and CEOs who report that they have not met their targets have been known to be summarily dismissed.

At one recent meeting in Munich, Mr. Bortolo announced that the company had decided that all subsidiaries should be funded to develop new inventory-control systems. The old systems were well past their use-by date, and were beginning to malfunction in most subsidiaries. He had commissioned a report from an independent consulting firm, which had examined solutions provided by a number of IT suppliers. Three new solutions had been found to be suitable, and Bortolo expected each subsidiary to adopt one of the three in the coming months. The most favored system was called Apex, but any of the three would be acceptable. Alessandro Bortolo was smart enough to realize that each subsidiary had its own special characteristics and that there was something to be said for allowing each to make its own decision. Accordingly, he recommended Apex but made it clear that the head office would support each national company in its own choice.

Tom Hammond had an information systems background and prided himself on being able to make a speedy rational assessment of IT solutions. Reading the briefing documents concerning the three solutions that night, he quickly concluded that for his subsidiary's configuration Apex was better than the two other alternatives and far superior to the system he was currently using. The next morning he advised Mr. Bortolo that his company would press ahead with Apex as soon as possible.

Tom also shared his view with Hoshi Yamamoto. Hoshi said, a little cautiously, that he agreed but did not want to rush things. The old system was still working in Tokyo and without too many problems. He intended to take the three solutions back to Japan and discuss them with his colleagues before coming to a decision. "I am sure," he said, "that we too will go with Apex. But there is no rush."

Back in Toronto, Tom announced the good news about the extra funding and the new, superior system. A few eyebrows were raised about the haste and the lack of consultation, but Tom used his IT know-how and presentation skills to persuade his staff that Apex would quickly boost the company's performance. He also found out a lot more about Apex. Over the next few months the IT people moved in and installed the new system. There were some teething problems and a few grumbles from the staff, but Tom thought, "That's what happens with any new system." Positive results, he was convinced, would soon come.

At the next six-monthly meeting, in Melbourne, Tom proudly announced that Apex was up and running. Most of the other subsidiaries had also decided to go with Apex, but the Canadian operation was the only one that had already installed it. Tom was surprised to find, however, that Hoshi and his Japanese team still had not made a decision. Mr. Bortolo was noticeably unimpressed by this delay and somewhat abruptly said that he hoped the Japanese would soon decide what they wanted. At dinner that night, Hoshi looked worried.

"My people will not agree with each other," he said. "I can't get them to a consensus. I don't know what to do."

"I know what I would do," said Tom. "Make a decision. Make the decision *you* think best. After all, you're the manager."

Back in Toronto, Tom faced another surprise. In his absence there had been an open revolt against Apex by a number of his key staff, a revolt that his deputy had not been able to quell. Three key people had handed in their resignations, and several others were dissatisfied. They agreed that Apex had been a technically superior solution but said that it had user-interface defects that made it almost impossible to work with. It should, they said, have been trialed before the decision was made. They felt they should have been involved.

Tom called in the systems installation company. He ran special coaching for staff. He counseled everyone to persevere with the new system: once they had gained confidence, everything would be fine. It did no good. Major problems continued, mostly caused, it seemed, by human error. More staff left. In no time at all, morale plummeted, errors multiplied, and the company's performance declined. Gloomily, Tom put the best gloss he could on his upcoming six-month report and flew to the meeting in London. He was not optimistic about how Mr. Bortolo would respond and wondered if he would keep his job.

He got to his London conference hotel the night before the meeting. At the bar, he caught sight of Hoshi, greeted him warmly, and bought him a drink. He was keen to find out whether his Japanese friend had also chosen Apex, and if so, how he had got on with it.

"Yes," said Hoshi. "They finally decided two months ago. They were unanimous. Having talked it through, everyone is very enthusiastic about the new system. It is being installed now." He hesitated. "Unfortunately, I think it is too late." He went on to explain how a major security malfunction of the old system had enabled a company fraudster to misappropriate several million dollars' worth of stock, ruining the company's half-year result.

Gloomily, Tom and Hoshi began to lay bets with each other as to which of them Bortolo would fire first the next day.

Decision making is the essence of the manager's job. Every management task involves choosing among alternatives. In this case Tom and Hoshi had to decide which inventory-control system to acquire. In planning, the manager must decide which strategy to follow; in organizing, which structure to adopt; in leading, which style to practice; in staffing, which candidate to select. Decisions change things—for good or bad. Managers' success depends in large measure on the consequences of their decisions. Later in this chapter we will see that Tom and Hoshi were adhering to decision models that were characteristic of their cultural backgrounds. Cultural intelligence would have enabled Tom and Hoshi to break out of their culturally based decision-making scripts, and if they had been mindful they might even have learned from each other.

The Rational Model

Decision making in many Western countries and organizations has been heavily influenced by the application of formal logic to business. The Western model of management tells us that decision making operates—or should operate—in a sequence of steps. Essentially these involve

- *defining a problem*: for example, a leadership vacuum created by the resignation of the organization's CEO
- *generating a range of potential solutions*: for example, attracting a range of candidates for the vacant CEO job

- *applying systematic analysis to the potential solutions to predict which will best satisfy predetermined criteria*: for example, subjecting candidates to formal assessments in an attempt to determine which would provide the best leadership if appointed
- *choosing and implementing the best alternative*: for example, selecting and appointing and supporting the candidate for CEO who performs best on the assessments[1]

This approach is the basis of management science and is implicit in the thinking behind such management decision-making techniques as linear programming, break-even analysis, feasibility studies, strategic choice, and personnel selection. Many managers pride themselves on their powers of reason and logic and typically promote and defend their decisions on this basis. However, other decision-making models are possible. What would you think of a board chair who said that the new CEO had been selected for one of the following reasons?

"His father had the job before him—it's a company tradition."

"We liked her more than any of the other candidates."

"He comes from a good family and attended an excellent university."

"We asked all the employees, and she got the most votes."

"We prayed, and God showed us the correct choice."

"We hired him because he is the brother of a board member."

"We all know him well, and we know we can trust him."

"Through his wife, he has excellent political connections."

"We chose her because she offered the biggest payment."

"I don't really know why we appointed him. It just seemed like the right thing to do. It was intuitive."

A board behaving in any of these ways in many Western countries might have its shareholders howling for blood. Yet in some parts of the world all of the criteria above are commonplace, and understood, and part of the fabric of business decision making. Even in the West they may be more common than we imagine—it's just that it wouldn't do to admit to them. Instead, those who make an appointment based on tradition, personal attractiveness, family background, popularity, nepotism, friendship, politics, graft, or intuition typically deny that these factors have anything to do with it and invent "rational" grounds for the decision.

This adherence to rational decision making—or at least a show of rational decision making—is of course part of a script or cultural cruise control, which we have described earlier in the book. In the case study with which we opened this chapter, rationality is part of the underlying philosophy of the Fresci Corporation and its Canadian manager, Tom Hammond. However, his Japanese counterpart, Hoshi Yamamoto, appears to be operating from different assumptions, with a script that elevates harmonious relationships and consensus above both rational decision making and speed in getting things done. Cultures often have different criteria against which to assess decision outcomes. In the event, both Tom and Hoshi were undone by failing to turn off their cultural cruise control and by sticking to their cultural scripts.

Can Western managers be sure that the rational way of thinking in which they are indoctrinated by their society, their education, and their companies is always the best basis for decision making? We think not. The world's diversity gives the West something to teach others about decision making and something to learn from them as well.

In this chapter we focus on the predominant rational model, indicate some limitations in its use, show some alternatives that are used effectively in other cultures, and advocate a more flexible, culturally intelligent approach to decision making based on appreciating and using a diversity of approaches.

Problems with the Rational Model

Quite apart from the alternatives used in non-Western cultures, it is well known that the rational model of decision making is imperfect.[2] It might work well if

- managers had clear unambiguous criteria to work toward (for example, short-term versus long-term profit, market share, employee safety, staff harmony). In fact, criteria are seldom clearly defined and often conflict with one another.

- managers were agreed on rational mental models to understand the human elements that are present in organizations. It is often easy to understand a mechanical or financial system in rational terms, but in systems involving people, even highly qualified behavioral scientists can seldom agree.

- managers were capable of accurately defining the problem in the first place, of generating a range of alternative solutions, accurately predicting the outcomes of all possible solutions, and manipulating huge amounts of relevant data. In fact, managers have limited capacity in the solutions they can generate, the predictions they can make, and the data they can handle.

- managers were unbiased enough to stick with the solution suggested by a rational analysis, even if they personally didn't like it.

- there were time to consider fully every possible alternative. Imagine, for example, trying to select a new home by evaluating every single house in the city.

Even managers who pride themselves on their rationality are seldom able to overcome these difficulties. In practice, managers adopt various decision-making strategies that are less than rational.

- They work *incrementally,* moving gradually toward a decision in small steps rather than performing a single powerful analysis.

- They create *heuristics,*[3] simple rules of thumb which may or may not have a rational basis but which simplify the decision-making task.

- They *satisfice;*[4] that is, they choose a plausible alternative that they become aware of early, rather than continuing to look for the best alternative.

- They procrastinate, they panic, and sometimes they avoid the decision altogether.

These characteristics of the ways managers make decisions are apparently consistent across cultures. All businesspeople simplify the rational decision-making process in predictable ways. However, because managers from different cultures have been programmed to see the world differently, they also differ in the ways they simplify the complex decision-making process.

For example, a common mental simplification (called *availability*) is to rely on how easy it is to recall something from memory and to make judgments about its frequency, probability, or likely cause. That is, an event easily imagined is given more weight in making a judgment. Because this *heuristic* is based on experience it can vary across cultures. It is probable, for example, that Thais would give a higher estimate of the worldwide rate of death by being trampled by a water buffalo than would Americans.

We have suggested that in some cultural settings decisions might be appropriate that are not based on rationality but on, say, tradition, or consensus, or family advantage, or custom. Even if we can get around all the impediments to rationality mentioned above, what it means to be rational differs across cultures, and a decision made without reference to cultural factors is at least as likely to fail as a decision made purely on cultural grounds.

One reason why rational decisions fail to be made and implemented is the problem of acceptability. It has been wisely stated that the measure of a decision's adequacy is a function of its quality and its acceptability.[5] Trying to approximate rationality (appropriate definition of the problem, accurate information, and a logical process for analyzing it) will often give a high-quality result. For example, we may be able to accurately predict the sales and profitability of a new product line.

But the decision not only has to be made, it also has to be *implemented,* usually by people other than the decision maker. In the case of the new product, the designers, product managers, marketers, and sales staff have to find the decision acceptable. If they do not, they will not be committed to making the decision work, and, however rational it is, it is likely to fail. In the case with which we opened this chapter, Tom Hammond's decision in favor of Apex may have been of high quality, but it was clearly of low acceptability to the staff members responsible for implementing it.

Culture imposes limits on what is acceptable and therefore on what decisions can realistically be implemented. In some countries the appointment of a woman to a high-status position—however well she may fit the criteria for the job—is unacceptable, so that even if the woman is appointed she will most likely fail because of the unwillingness of those around her to work with her. In other countries the implementation of work practices and schedules that involve breaking religious taboos cannot be tolerated, no matter how rational they may be.

One of the most important limitations on rational decision making comes from the cultural dimension, identified in Chapter 2, called *collectivism.* Collectivism calls into question not what the decision is, but how the decision is made and who makes it. In an individualistic culture it is acceptable for an individual to make decisions, particularly if the society also has a norm of hierarchy and the decision maker has formal authority. But in a collectivist culture it is expected that the collective will be properly informed, consulted, and involved. This is why Hoshi Yamamoto, in the opening case, was so reluctant to make the decision he favored in his collectivist Japanese organization. Rational logic may be fine in a collectivist culture—provided everyone has the chance to contribute to the logic and to ponder and discuss whether it actually works.

We cannot emphasize strongly enough how important it is for Western managers to suspend, in part, their own belief in rationality as the basis for business decision making and to be mindful of the specifics affecting decision making in other cultures. They may then be able to figure out how to reinterpret rationality to accommodate habits and constraints that are an important part of the local culture. Again, the scripts of rational decision making must be suppressed and cruise control must be switched off.

Motivation and Goals

In addition to the process of mental simplification described above, business decisions are affected by the motives and goals of those who make them.[6] For example, a manager deciding whom to appoint as her assistant might be motivated by the desire to improve the organization's performance, the desire to remain popular with staff, the need to maintain power by appointing a weak subordinate, the wish to follow tradition, or any of a number of other factors. Such motives vary with culture. Individual needs reflect cultural values.

In many Western cultures, would-be rational decision makers pride themselves on their ability to set aside their personal motivations when they make decisions, and to rely instead on applying logic to achieve the result that will be best for the company. Thus, they will choose the candidate they think will do the job best, rather than the one they like the most. The non-Western alternative to the rational model might be labeled the motivational model, in which individuals are, in a sense more honestly, driven by their own motives, values, traditions, and habits. These frequently have a cultural basis.

For example, the motivation for personal dominance and

power is affected by the cultural dimension power distance (Chapter 2), which is high, for example, in Latin America but low in Scandinavian countries, Israel, and Australasia. Similarly, individualism (characteristic of the United States and many Western countries) is associated with need for achievement, while collectivism (characteristic of Latin America and many Asian countries) usually involves high need for affiliation (close personal relationships). Collectivism also reflects a worldview in which people are seen as interdependent with others, whereas in individualist cultures they are defined as independent.

A fundamental difference like this individualist-collectivist dichotomy can dramatically affect business and political decisions. When British prime minister Margaret Thatcher famously remarked that "there is no such thing as society," she was making an exceptionally powerful statement of the individualist view at the heart of her attempts to foster a political and business system based on individual enterprise.

People from individualist cultures generally assert their own rights and ideas and resist group pressure, whereas those from collectivist cultures are more influenced by the context and the ideas of the other people involved. For example, in one research study,[7] people from collectivist Brazil were more likely than those from individualistic United States to forego a personal financial benefit in order to visit a sick friend. Another important product of individualism is high individual self-esteem and optimism. For example, Americans are much more likely to overestimate their abilities, chances of success, and so on, than are the collectivist Japanese. But Japanese are more likely to believe that their judgments are shared by others.[8]

Culture also determines what will be acceptable to people in management practice. Individual incentives for productivity may get good results in an individualist culture but not in a collectivist one. In a high power distance culture, employees expect and may even welcome relatively autocratic behavior from managers, but in a low power distance culture, they will reject such behavior. Managers need to be mindful and to have the skill to read the motivation of staff, particularly where that motivation is culturally based.

In addition, by considering culturally based motivational differences, managers may be better able to understand the decision-making methods and criteria used by their counterparts with different cultural backgrounds. Tom and Hoshi, in the opening case in this chapter, epitomize the individualist and collectivist nature of their respective cultures. Each acted according to the motivation of his cultural group. Both failed to exhibit cultural intelligence. Their failures can be attributed both to lack of knowledge and to failure to be mindful. Tom, acting according to his mental programming, was too autocratic in his process for choosing the new system, while Hoshi, in respecting the need for collective action, did not use his authority to ensure the group made a timely decision.

Selection and Allocation Decisions

IT'S WHO YOU KNOW THAT COUNTS

Jan Moore, the European area manager for Clarkson Equipment Corporation (CEC), was frustrated with the human resource management situation at CEC's joint venture in Russia. She contacted Craig Finley, CEC's country manager for Russia, to remind him that a human resource manager was supposed to have been hired three years ago, as soon as the joint venture was official. The Russian joint venture manager Alexandr (Sasha) Lebedeva had decided to manage the HR function himself.

As a result, all of the venture's senior managers had been appointed by the Russian partner. Additionally, quite a few of the senior managers' relatives had also been hired. The worst case, Jan believed, was that Sasha's son had already built an astonishing career within twelve months, starting as an assistant, becoming purchasing manager, and then being sent to Western Europe for eighteen months' practical training.

Unhappy with Sasha's hiring practices, Jan had instructed Craig to introduce CEC's standard hiring practices, which had been developed by the European headquarters. These included preparing job requisitions, advertising vacant positions, evaluating candidates' résumés, and having line managers conduct interviews. These had been introduced, but the Russian managers had ignored the procedures. For example, Jan discovered that just one week earlier a new machine operator had been hired for the factory without Craig's knowledge. He turned out to be the inexperienced eighteen-year-old son of a local customs officer who often cleared shipments for CEC.

When Jan confronted Craig about the matter, she got a rather philosophical reply: "Well, you have to remember the specifics of the country you are operating in. Russia has an Asian culture and European faces should not mislead you. Western standards do not always work here. If hiring people you have known for a long time and therefore trust is a local custom, you can't change it overnight. And you probably don't need to change it."[9]

Staff selection decisions are among the most common a manager has to make. In the example, the westerners, as usual, proposed a rational model in the assessment of candidates, focusing on behavior. The Russians preferred to rely on more subtle and traditional cues of suitability for the job.

One way of understanding these differences is to contrast the Western view that what counts is *what you can do* with the Eastern belief that it is *who you are* that matters. In China, the network of a candidate's relationships, his or her *guanxi*,[10] can be critical to selection for a job. In the West, this is thought of as favoritism or nepotism, and is frowned upon: candidates, rather than relying on their connections, are expected to demonstrate their personal suitability for the job. The East-West difference may be made worse by the current Western fashion—often built in to local legislation—for equal employment opportunity—meaning opportunity based solely on the Western criteria of individually demonstrated ability to do the job.

Other cultural differences in selection practice are more subtle. In one recent research study conducted in Europe,[11] the ability to do the job was the main criterion across a number of countries, but "ability" was very differently defined, with egalitarian Scandinavian countries putting a lot of emphasis on interpersonal skills, whereas countries emphasizing status differences paid more attention to age.

Reward-allocation decisions require the making of decisions that balance equality against equity. Suppose several people collaborate to complete a project, but some use more skill, work longer hours, and make more effort than others. An equitable allocation of rewards will distribute them in relation to responsibility, time, effort, and so on. An equal allocation of rewards will reward all participants equally just for contributing. Individualist cultures of course favor equitable solutions, and collectivist cultures equal ones. Collectivists are also more likely to take into account need as a criterion for reward allocation.

Consider the problem of distributing a bonus among several employees with equal tenure. One is clearly the hardest worker and the most important contributor, another is a high-status, wealthy person with powerful connections that could be helpful in the future, and another has recently had a family tragedy and has considerable additional expenses. Which of these people is most deserving of a bonus? How would you distribute a fixed bonus amount among them? Should your decision be based primarily on equity, equality, or need? Which of your assumptions are based on values and beliefs that are associated with your culture? Can you see how someone with different assumptions might allocate rewards differently?

Ethics and Decision Making

In the global business environment virtually every decision has an ethical component. The business and political press tell us regularly of ongoing ethical crises in many countries: for example, a continuing flow of business executives lining their pockets through the pillaging of their companies; lies and deception practiced against shareholders; "pork-barrel" politics; and systematic bribery and corruption in the governmental institutions of many countries. The following are examples of common business decisions that present global managers with ethical dilemmas:

- Moving production to a foreign country to take advantage of cheap labor.
- Discouraging union organizing in countries where unions are not well established.
- Abiding only by the minimum environmental protection laws imposed by the country in which you are operating.
- Transferring to foreign investors assets that belong to the country as a whole.
- Speculating against your own country's currency.
- Trading on the black market to avoid currency controls on repatriation of profits.
- Promoting dangerous products in a foreign market when demand declines at home.
- Doing business in a country with a repressive government.
- Using data collected by the clandestine operations of a government for business advantage.
- Exporting harmful substances that are illegal in a company's home country but not in the host country.
- Licensing production in a country in order to prevent paying bribes directly.
- Imposing a global ethical norm developed by the headquarters of the firm.
- Advertising luxury goods in less developed countries (LDCs).
- Establishing transfer prices to minimize global tax payments and maximize cash flows.

You don't have to be at the top of the organization to face ethical dilemmas in your decision making. Whether to pay unofficial inducements, what level of expenses to claim, and whether to accept gifts from prospective suppliers—all raise ethical questions. Those doing business internationally quickly realize that what they think is morally correct erodes in the face of differing cultural values and norms for behavior. It is often difficult to reconcile one's own ethical standards with local practices, and it is often very difficult to say no when invited to do something one truly believes to be wrong.

The reason is that many business decisions are ethically ambiguous. Consider the common decision of firms in economically advanced countries to relocate manufacturing in developing countries in order to achieve lower labor costs. Here is how such a decision might be perceived by (a) a manager from a developed country making such a decision in order to keep his company in business and (b) an activist concerned about the welfare of the people in the developing world.

> *Businessman:* "If we do not make this decision, we will go out of business, and everyone will lose their jobs, not just those in our European factory. We would be bringing to the people of the region in China where we seek to set up our factory an opportunity to participate in the Western dream of secure employment. We will pay a competitive wage to attract their labor. No one will force anybody to work for us — they will do it because they know they are better off that way. We are helping them! But we cannot pay more. That would enable our competitors to take our market away, and everyone would suffer, including our Chinese employees. Our extension to China, you see, is totally ethical."

> *Activist:* "Your company is a fundamentally immoral organization, interested only in generating huge profit for its managers and shareholders. It seeks to move into China only because it knows it can exploit the people there. It will pay them wages that they can scarcely live on, force them to work long hours, and neglect their health and safety needs. If the company

really wants to help the Chinese people, why doesn't it double the proposed wages and ensure reasonable working conditions? It could do that and still make a huge profit. But multinationals don't think this way, because they are fundamentally unethical."

Who is right? Both! The two protagonists are proceeding from very different frames of reference. Interestingly, though, each party is seeking to do right by the Chinese workers involved.

To the activist, the concept of profit appears inherently immoral. Her questioning is part of a radical analysis of "big business" that focuses particularly on multinational companies because they use intercountry differences in areas such as labor costs, pollution control, and ability to get their way with government authorities as a basis for making big decisions—such as relocation—in the "rational" interest of profitability. This is part of a wider belief by businesspeople that in the end striving for profit is good for everyone—including the Chinese workers—because it causes economic systems to become more and more efficient and makes goods cheaper. While, as we shall see, different cultures tend to have different views of business freedom and control, the moral questions separating the businessman in our example from the activist cut across cultural boundaries, and the attitudes and institutions that support them are international.

The previously described situation is an example of perhaps the most difficult ethical dilemma that global managers face. It is essentially the question "Should I follow a practice that is allowed in a foreign country, but not in my own?" There are three ways that managers commonly try to answer this question.[12]

- The first of these tries to evaluate the consequences of the decision and calculates the maximum benefit for the most people. This is what the businessman was arguing in defense of moving his factory to China. Many Chinese people would benefit, as well as the businessman's own shareholders. However, as indicated by the response of the activist, benefit is often in the eye of the beholder.

- The second approach is to rely on some moral rule. We all learn such rules as part of our cultural socialization, and these rules are often apparent in religious teachings. An example is the idea of treating others as you would like to be treated. However, the obvious problem with moral rules is finding a set of rules upon which all cultures can agree. For example, even in cultures as similar as the United States and Canada, strong differences in opinion exist with regard to the right of the state to put someone to death.

- The final method of answering ethical questions is the culturally relative approach. This approach suggests that ethical behavior varies from one culture to the next. While seemingly consistent with our general recommendations for being culturally intelligent, this approach is also insufficient to deal with the ethical dilemmas of global managers attempting to make decisions across cultural boundaries. While many differences in business practice are in fact related to the cultural norms of a society, cultural relativity can make it possible for people to justify truly reprehensible behavior based on culture.

What then is the global manager who wants to make an ethical decision to do? Not surprisingly, we suggest that the steps to cultural intelligence will also lead to more ethical decision making across cultures.

The first step is *knowledge*. You need to understand your own mental programming with regard to what is ethical. What do you believe is proper behavior and why do you believe it? You also need an awareness that people in other cultures hold a variety of values that are relative to their society.

The second step is being *mindful* of the ethical component of decisions. Who is likely to benefit and who will be harmed by the decision? In this case, mindfulness also means paying attention to all the factors that might influence the decision.

These include the relative level of economic development in a society. The mindful manager will ask, "Would this practice be acceptable in my country at a similar level of economic development? Is this practice a violation of some fundamental human right?"[13]

The *behavioral skills* of the culturally intelligent manager will include a repertoire of behaviors that recognize value differences across cultures but are consistent with self-chosen ethical principles. These principles will develop over time as the manager gains more knowledge and practices mindfulness. He or she will uphold these nonrelative values and rights regardless of majority opinion and will act in accord with these principles. Doing so will often require creative solutions to ethical dilemmas. For example, one company, while yielding to the cultural norm of employing children under the age of fifteen in its manufacturing process in a developing country, also provided time off and monetary support to allow these children to acquire a basic education.

Summary

This chapter describes the global manager's role as a decision maker. It may be that the world is gradually accepting a Western-style rational approach to decision making, but this approach is far from universal. Globalization is itself a strategy that is driven by a relentless logic of business profitability, and the process of globalization has been led and dominated by organizations based in the United States and Western European countries attempting to impose that logic in Latin America, Asia, Eastern Europe, and the Middle East. However, because people in different cultures have different mental programming, the ways in which they simplify the complex process of decision making also differ. Even in attempting a rational process, the ways they define a problem, generate, weight, and select alternatives is likely to be different. Also, decisions are affected by the motives and goals of the decision maker, which are based on culturally different values. The culturally intelligent manager is better able to understand the decision-making methods and criteria used in other cultures. Virtually all business decisions have an ethical component, because some stakeholders benefit and others do not. The culturally intelligent manager is able to balance the culturally relative nature of business ethics while upholding fundamental human rights.

CHAPTER 6

Communicating and Negotiating Across Cultures

Consider these four vignettes of cross-cultural living, all of them authentic experiences involving Americans.[1]

- An American HR manager works for a multinational in Brazil. His role in recruitment of local staff makes him a target for job-seekers. At a party, a female Brazilian acquaintance tells him she wants to introduce a female friend to him. The friend, she says, "is very interested in your company." The American acquiesces, saying "I just hope I don't get hustled." To his surprise, his friend excuses herself and does not speak to him again.

- An American student shares a dormitory room with a Thai. They have similar routines and interests, and get on well. Then, after several weeks of living together, the Thai abruptly announces that he has applied for a transfer to another room. The American is surprised and upset and asks the Thai why he wants to move. The Thai is reluctant to speak but eventually says that he can't stand the American's noisiness, loud stereo, late visitors and untidiness. The American is even more surprised: all this is new to him.

"Couldn't you have told me this sooner?" he says. "Maybe I could have done something about it."

- A newly qualified American community counselor is assigned as a client a Malaysian man who suffers from low energy and poor concentration. In their first interview the Malaysian is very quiet and withdrawn. The counselor is used to silences in counseling sessions, as clients reflect and analyze, but this client does not seem to want to communicate at all. So the counselor takes time to try to persuade him of the nature of the counseling process. At the end of the session the client does not seek any further counseling. The counselor is disappointed: he has learned almost nothing about his client. Has he done something wrong?

- An American economist is on a study tour in China. He visits an economic planning institute where a Chinese economist, who is interested in the American's economic forecasting techniques, invites him to spend two months in China giving seminars. The American is very interested in the offer, and says so, but adds that he has to check with the administration of his U.S. institute to get their approval. Back in the United States, he is granted the necessary clearance and sends a message to China indicating that he is definitely available. But the Chinese never contact him again.

These cases, to which we will return later, demonstrate communication failures that led to the breakdown of relationships, and all have cultural origins.

Communication—the interchange of messages between people—is the fundamental building block of social experience. Whether selling, buying, negotiating, leading, or working with others, we communicate. And although the idea of communicating a message seems simple and straightforward— "You just tell it straight, right? And you listen."—when it comes to figuring out what goes wrong in life, "communication failure" is by far the most common explanation of all.

Basically, communication operates through *codes*—systems of signs in which each sign signifies a particular idea or concept.

Communication also uses *conventions*—agreed-upon norms about how, when, and in what context codes will be used. If two different people do not share the same codes and conventions they will have difficulty communicating with each other. And codes and conventions are determined in large measure by people's cultures. The most obvious example of nonshared codes is different languages.

Each communication breakdown in our opening set of vignettes can be explained in terms of cultural differences:

- The HR manager who didn't want to be "hustled" had a verbal misunderstanding. When he said, "I hope I don't get hustled," he meant he hoped that the person he was being introduced to would not try to persuade him to offer her a job. But in Latin countries the term "hustle" is more likely to refer to making romantic or sexual advances. His female acquaintance felt he was being rude in suggesting that her friend might behave in such a way. This is an example of different *codes*.

- In the case of the student whose Thai friend moved out, culture and custom interfered with communication. In their upbringing, Americans are encouraged to be active, assertive, and open, and they expect the same in others. In *their* upbringing, Thais are encouraged to be passive and sensitive, and they too expect the same in others. The Thai student expected the American to be sensitive to his feelings; the American expected the Thai to be upfront by saying what his feelings were. When neither behaved as he was expected to, the relationship broke down. This is an example of different *conventions*.

- The counselor whose Malaysian client wouldn't talk failed to appreciate the meaning of an important part of the communication—the silences! Silences are not always absence of communication; they are often *part* of communication. Asians tend to wait longer than Westerners before speaking, especially if the person they are talking to is an authority figure. To some extent the length of silences is a sign of respect. The counselor might have been more patient. Also, the Malaysian would likely not have been assertive enough to seek another appointment without being invited. So the whole situation was mismanaged. This is an example of different *codes* AND *conventions*.

- The economist whose invitation to visit China was never followed up failed to appreciate the meaning of his own communication in Chinese culture. A Chinese saying that he had to check with his office before accepting the invitation might have been communicating two things: first, that he was a relatively low-status person who had to check with bureaucrats before making a decision; second, that he was politely indicating that he was not really interested in visiting. Even when the answer Chinese people want to give is "no," they seldom say so directly. Instead, they have numerous polite ways—including the one in this story—of courteously indicating it. This is another example of different *codes* AND *conventions*.

How Communication Works

In communication, the communicator transmits messages to others ("receivers") who interpret them. The process is shown in Figure 6.1.

Often the receiver in turn becomes the communicator, and the process is reversed. The channel may be spoken words, written words, or nonverbal behavior such as gestures or facial expressions. Face-to-face conversations, meetings, telephone calls, letters, other written documents, or e-mail may all be used. Successful communication occurs when the message is accurately perceived and understood. Such factors as skills of communicating and listening, selection of an appropriate channel, and the absence of "interference" from competing messages and other factors are all important. Cultural differ-

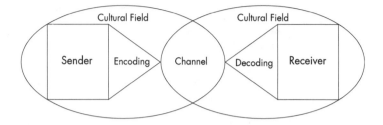

FIGURE 6.1. Cross-cultural communication process

ences threaten communication because they reduce the availability of codes and conventions that are shared by sender and receiver.

The cultural field shown in Figure 6.1 represents culturally based elements in the sender's and in the receiver's background, such as their language, education and values.[2] The cultural field creates the *codes* used in the encoding and decoding process and the cultural *conventions* that affect the communication process.

Language

Language is the most obvious code into which senders encode messages and from which receivers decode them. In language, particular combinations of sounds are arbitrarily chosen to represent elements of meaning and can thereby be used to represent complex messages. In addition, most languages contain speech conventions, subtleties, and figures of speech, of which only experienced speakers may be aware. For example, in English "fleshpots" literally means the same as "pans of meat," yet a person experienced in the language perceives and uses a completely different interpretation, possibly to the puzzlement of learners.

The essence of language is that sender and receiver should share the code. The problem is that the process of human evolution has left us with thousands of different languages, plus different dialects and adaptations of many of them.[3] Nearly all individuals have only one first language, which they have learned and spoken from early childhood, and even the most accomplished linguist will be fluent in only a few. Moreover, psychologists have determined that the best time to acquire new languages is before the age of ten, after which we become progressively less able to make this adaptation.[4]

The situation is complicated by the fact that whatever the language, its everyday use, in business as elsewhere, goes beyond any simple single code that one might find, for example, in a dictionary. Languages are living entities that grow and change to accommodate the widely different groups who use them and the changes in the social circumstances in which they are used. For example, among young Americans, language is becoming more dramatic, so that

> "She accused me of breaking the window. I said I hadn't."

has become:

> "She's like, 'you trashed the window!' I'm like, 'No way it was me!'"

In most cultures, different groups have their own vocabularies, slang, jargon, and idioms. Sometimes the differences are so strong and systematic that we call this variation a different dialect. In addition, technical or social groups may develop their own jargon and either must be careful to provide translation for outsiders, or may use the jargon to distance themselves from outsiders. Another common linguistic convention is euphemism, when words with sexual or other potentially impolite connotations are replaced with less explicit words. For example, in some English-speaking cultures it is common to say that someone has "passed away" instead of saying the person has "died."

Finally, most of us would be surprised at the extent to which we mindlessly use proverbs, maxims, and even slogans or catchphrases heard on television as part of our day-to-day conversation. Examples are the Anglo-American expressions "he pulled the wool over my eyes," "the greatest thing since sliced bread," and "not on the same wavelength." Such expressions are in good English but may genuinely puzzle outsiders. The following is an example of such mindlessness in communication by a newcomer to a Russian manufacturing plant.

THE SAFETY EXPERT

An American safety expert came to the St. Petersburg plant to address a big meeting of all employees. I asked him to tell the interpreter what he would say, not to surprise the interpreter, and to say very little and *not* go into lots of detail. The expert stood up, hands on hips, and pointed to the man on the floor in front of him, and said, "How would you like to lose a foot?"

The translator translated, literally. The audience looked surprised. No one knew where this was going.

Then he said,

"Sell me your hand, what's it cost?"

The translator obediently repeated it in Russian. The audience looked stunned.

All he was trying to do was to dramatize the costs of accidents. And he was concise, just like I'd asked him. But too much got lost in the translation. The whole thing was a disaster. I tried to do damage control. It took a month for the safety expert to realize he'd blown it; no one listened to him in meetings, and employees avoided him.[5]

Finding Common Language Codes

It should be apparent that while language is a wonderful tool for communication, it is also fraught with difficulties. If two people seeking to communicate with each other do not have any overlapping language codes, they face a major barrier. They can, of course, resort to employing translators. Translators are skilled in more than one language and adept at restating a message in a different language so that the receiver can readily understand it. But translation is time-consuming and expensive. It also complicates the communication process and potentially distorts the message by requiring a further transformation of it. Many businesspeople therefore recognize the advantages of having a shared language.

If you do choose to learn and use a foreign language, you may find benefits beyond simply overcoming the language barrier. Most people appreciate the efforts that others may have made to learn their language. So, even though your fluency in another language may be limited—sometimes so limited that a person from the other culture may immediately try to find an alternative shared language—the fact that you have made the effort may generate goodwill.[6] In addition, language conveys many subtleties about a culture that a person with high cultural intelligence might notice and use.

However, learning a new language carries major costs. It takes substantial study and practice to become fluent in another language, particularly if that language is unlike your own in pronunciation, grammatical structure, and conventions. Not only must you expend considerable time and effort in learning, you must also accept that when using the language you will be under more stress than when using your own language, and you may even be distracted from other aspects of the situation. Also, your lack of fluency in the new language may in some cases unfairly undermine your credibility in the eyes of fluent speakers. But in other instances, fluency may lead to your being perceived as being competent (more competent than you actually are) in other areas, such as overall cultural intelligence.[7]

Second Language Use

One by-product of the Anglo-American business dominance of the twentieth century and the relentless unwillingness of British and American people to learn languages other than their own has been to make English increasingly the accepted common language of business organizations and businesspeople. Worldwide, the learning of English to facilitate international communication has become a major activity. This situation hugely facilitates processes of international communication in business. Those who speak English as their first language owe a debt to the millions of people round the world who have gone out of their way to help out with an international problem by learning to understand, read, speak, and write in the English language.

Learning English as a second language (ESL) is full of challenges. Its richness of vocabulary (for example, it has over 200,000 words in common use as compared to 100,000 in French) and its numerous synonyms (English is the only language with books of synonyms like *Roget's Thesaurus*) can cause ESL speakers great difficulty. Take the simple word "fly." It can mean an annoying insect, a means of travel, or an important part of men's trousers.[8]

In communicating with a nonnative English speaker, the person fluent in English has an obligation to ensure clear, simple communication by communicating in relatively standard terms, by avoiding jargon and other obscure language, and by not making too many assumptions about comprehension by the other person. Culturally intelligent people will consciously adapt their own style of language to be in harmony with the vocabulary and style of the other person—a good example of following the knowledge–mindfulness–behavioral skills model outlined in Chapters 2 and 3.

Some ESL speakers—particularly those from cultures that set high store by not losing face—respond to the situation by pretending to understand when they really do not, further interfering with good communication. In these situations there is a special onus on the parties to attend closely to the communication process, to be aware of barriers and limitations in their sending and receiving of messages, and to check whether messages have successfully got through.

The following are some brief guidelines that culturally intelligent businesspeople can use to help improve communication with ESL speakers.

Second-Language Strategies

- Use clear, slow speech. Enunciate carefully and avoid colloquial expressions
- Repeat important points using different words to explain the same concept.
- Use active verbs and avoid long compound sentences.
- Use visual restatements such as pictures, graphs, tables, and slides.
- Hand out written summaries of your verbal presentation.
- Pause more frequently, and do not jump in to fill silences.
- Take frequent breaks and allow more time.
- Be careful not to attribute poor grammar or mispronunciation to lack of intelligence.
- Check for understanding and comprehension by encouraging ESL speakers to repeat concepts back to you.
- Avoid embarrassing ESL speakers, but encourage and reinforce their participation.[9]

Conventions

Communication conventions cover the ways that language and other codes are used within a particular culture. Once again cultural values and norms, such as those based on collectivism or individualism are apparent.

EXPLICIT AND IMPLICIT COMMUNICATION

There is a Western convention that communication should be verbal and that verbal messages should be explicit, direct, and unambiguous—we should "tell it like it is" or "call a spade a spade." This arises in part from the Western view that individuals perceive something called the truth and should state it. But in other cultures—for example, many Middle Eastern and Asian cultures—there is no absolute truth, and politeness and desire to avoid embarrassment often take precedence. The convention is therefore that communication is implicit, indirect, and ambiguous. Here is an example:

WERE YOU FISHING IN THE ZONE?

A young New Zealand businessman, David Irving, of the food-processing company Wattie's, was assigned to find out from his company's Japanese joint-venture partner whether there was any truth in a New Zealand government allegation that the Japanese had been fishing within New Zealand's 200-mile illegal zone. Irving reports that he was direct in his approach:

"Were you fishing in the zone?"

I received an obscure, incomprehensible reply, but eventually I was able to ask again:

"Were you fishing in the zone?"

Again the answer was obscure. Morning tea came, and, during the break, one of the Japanese sidled up to me with what appeared to be an even more obscure statement:

"Irving-san, when you have dust in the corner of a room, it is hard to get it out."

I agreed, but didn't see the relevance. Negotiations resumed, and I asked for a third time:

"Were you fishing in the zone?"

The answer was more obscure than ever. We were getting nowhere. We adjourned for lunch. Again the Japanese sidled up to me.

"Irving-san, when you beat a mat, the dust will rise."

I thought about this, and at last understood. Japanese lose face when they acknowledge wrongdoing; therefore they avoid doing so directly and rely instead on obscurity. Their aphorisms were, however, an indirect admission of guilt.[10]

In the direct convention of communication, most of the message is placed in the *content* of the communication—the actual words that are used. In the indirect convention, the *context* is more important—for example, the physical setting, the previous relationships between the participants, and the nonverbal behavior of those involved.

The direct convention tends to be the norm in countries with highly individualistic cultures, the indirect in countries with collectivist cultures, where, perhaps, communicators need to be more cautious in expressing ideas. Nevertheless, understanding apparently indirect communication may sometimes be simply a matter of learning another code. The examples in the following box show a variety of ways of saying "no" politely and indirectly. In most cases a low CQ individual would understandably think that the answer was quite possibly "yes."

SAYING "NO" IN RESPONSE TO
"HAS MY PROPOSAL BEEN ACCEPTED?"[11]

Conditional "yes"	If everything proceeds as planned, the proposal will be approved.
Counter-question	Have you submitted a copy of your proposal to the ministry of . . . ?
Criticizing the question	Your question is very difficult to answer.
Refusing the question	We cannot answer this question at this time.
Tangential reply	Will you be staying longer than you had originally planned?
Yes, but	Yes, approval looks likely, but . . .
Delayed answer	You should know shortly.

The problems associated with explicitness of communication are of course not limited to face-to-face communication. In fact, the use of e-mail as the preferred mode of communication in many firms can make these problems even more difficult. One Dutch manager (direct convention) was so frustrated in trying to understand the real message in critical e-mails about a client relationship from his Mexican counterpart (indirect convention) that he finally jumped on an airplane and flew from Amsterdam to Mexico City just to get clarification.[12]

VERBOSITY AND SILENCE

Different cultures vary in their conventions about *how much* and *how loudly* one should talk. Americans are notorious for talking a lot and talking loudly. Silence can be used deliberately and strategically in communication. Japanese negotiators use silence as a means of controlling negotiating processes, whereas Finns use it as a way of encouraging a speaker to continue. As the counselor in one of our opening vignettes failed to note, in Malaysia silence can be used to show respect. Interpreting silence accurately is a key element in culturally intelligent communication.

Non-verbal Communication: Codes and Conventions

The topic of body language is popular, and most of us now realize that we communicate, often inadvertently, by such means as physical proximity and orientation to another person, body movements, gestures, facial expression, eye contact, and tone of voice. While claims that a skilled observer of nonverbal communication can "read other people like a book" or "know exactly what others are thinking" are exaggerated, there is no doubt that nonverbal communication supplements verbal communication a great deal.

Often, nonverbal communication is a good guide to the truth: for example, if an athlete is sitting in the dressing room after the match with his shoulders slumped, his arms folded, and the ends of his mouth turned down, you do not need to ask, whatever his culture, whether his team won or lost. Sometimes nonverbal behavior reveals the opposite of verbal— as, for example, when someone red in the face and obviously making a considerable effort to control himself, tells you, "No, I'm *not* angry."

Cross-cultural nonverbal communication is valuable because many nonverbal signals are similar between different cultures. For example, smiling universally expresses positive feelings. However, there are also subtle variations between cultures: for example Asians often smile to conceal nervousness or embarrassment. Even the casual observer has probably noticed giggling-behind-the-hand behavior by young Asian women when they are embarrassed. A shake of the head means disagreement in Western cultures but agreement in some parts of India. The codes that tell us the meanings of postures or gestures sometimes agree across cultures, but sometimes disagree. The conventions that tell us where to stand or whether to bow also vary.

DISTANCE

How close should you stand to other people when communicating with them? Should you face people directly, or stand beside them? Perhaps you have never thought about it and just let it come naturally. Also, the answer can vary according to the characteristics of the other person, for example, his or her authority, age, or gender. But there are certainly differences among cultures in terms of the distance at which people feel comfortable communicating. For example, in casual conversation, Greeks stand much closer than Americans, who stand much closer than Norwegians, and so on. A culturally intelligent person will be mindful of the comfort of those he or she deals with, and will possibly modify his or her social distance accordingly.[13]

TOUCHING

Should you ever touch the person you are communicating with? If so, where, and how much? In most cultures, touching another person symbolizes various emotions and relationships. The most obvious example is the handshake, which in many cultures denotes a friendly relationship—"I'm pleased to meet you" or "Goodbye for now." Kissing another person's cheek is common between men as well as women in France but much less so in America. In New Zealand the Maori greeting is the *hongi*, a firm pressing together of noses. In some cultures, approval or support may be shown by a slap on the back or a squeeze of the arm. Soccer players worldwide hug each other fiercely when their team scores a goal.

Because of gender differences and concerns about the sexual connotations of touching, conventions are often different for men and women. Knowing when and on what part of the body one can appropriately touch another person, requires a high level of cultural intelligence. However there are low-touch cultures (predominantly in North America, Northern Europe and Asia) and high-touch cultures (predominantly in Latin America, Southern and Eastern Europe, and the Middle East). A touch that is meant to be meaningful in the United States, such as a pat on the back, might not even be noticed in a high-touch culture like Brazil.

BODY POSITION

In a case in Chapter 1, a Samoan job applicant sat down in the office of an American senior manager, wanting, as is the norm in Samoa, to show respect by positioning himself at a physically lower level than the manager. But the gesture misfired because to Americans sitting down when others are standing is a sign of disrespect. Polite Americans wait for others to sit down before they do, and they show respect by rising from their seats when others enter the room. The way people position themselves has meaning in all cultures, but it is hard to draw up any hard-and-fast rules.

Another common body-position issue is the adoption of a position that makes one's body look big—for example a rigid, angular stance to denote aggression, or a curled-up and cowering posture to indicate submissiveness.[14] Bowing to show deference is common and understood across many cultures, but in some its use is extreme. For example, in Japan some stores employ people especially to bow to customers, but the (unwritten) rules about who should bow to whom and how exactly they should do it are complex, subtle, and difficult for even a culturally intelligent outsider to master. In fact, the culturally intelligent person knows that bowing in this manner is a custom best reserved for native Japanese and that trying to mimic it is at best humorous and at worst offensive.

GESTURES

Hand and arm movements are often used simply as physical accompaniments to words, to supplement them or to provide a visual illustration of what is being said. Often gestures are meaningless without the verbal commentary, other than as a general statement of the state of mind of the person. But there are also gestures that carry established meanings, for example pointing to indicate direction, hands held up with the palms facing upwards and outwards to indicate defensiveness, and a shrug of the shoulders to indicate incomprehension or lack of interest. Other more complex signals vary across cultures. Because some gestures that are positive, humorous, or harmless in some cultures are considered hostile, offensive, or obscene in other cultures, high CQ people avoid explicit gestures in other cultures until they know *exactly* what they mean.

FACIAL EXPRESSION

Facial expressions most obviously indicate the basic human emotions: happiness, surprise, disgust, fear, anger, and sadness. The facial expressions denoting these are instinctive and common across cultures.[15] However, in most cultures, people have learned how to disguise their emotions by adopting an expression that does not represent how they really feel. For example, do you truly believe that the flight attendant beaming happily at every passenger she serves is truly happy to meet each one? In some Asian cultures, smiling is often used to hide displeasure, sadness, or anger.

Emotions can also be concealed by the adoption of a neutral expression. Every negotiator and card player knows the value of being able to sit with a poker face devoid of any expression that might indicate to others how he or she is feeling about the offer that has just been made or about the cards that have just been dealt. Thus, while natural facial expressions provide a *code* to others' emotions that is common across cultures, in many situations *conventions* governing the use of facial expression can mean that facial cues are either absent or misleading. For example, in collectivist cultures, the open expression of individual emotion is often suppressed because it may threaten group harmony. This is one reason why westerners often characterize Chinese and Japanese people as inscrutable.

EYE CONTACT

Making eye contact with others (or avoiding eye contact) is another important form of nonverbal communication. In Western countries, for example, a moderate level of eye contact during conversation is a way of communicating friendliness or interest, whereas excessive eye contact (staring) is considered rude, and lack of eye contact is hostile. Eye contact is also used in conversation as a signal: for example, making eye contact with the other person as you finish a sentence often means, "Now it's your turn to speak."

Again, there are major cultural differences. Arabs, Latinos, Indians, and Pakistanis all have conventions of longer eye contact, whereas Africans and East Asians interpret eye contact as conveying anger or insubordination and avoid it. The situation is further complicated by the fact that most cultures have different conventions about eye contact depending on the gender, status, and so on of those involved.

With eye contact, as with other areas of nonverbal communication, the ability to observe the behavior of others, to be mindful of it and to reflect on it, and to be skilled at modifying one's own behavior in response, is a key component of cultural intelligence.

Negotiating Across Cultures

Negotiation is a special communication situation, one that is of particular importance in cross-cultural business settings, in which the objective is often for people to overcome conflicting interests and to reach an agreement that is advantageous to both parties. Books have been written on the characteristics and skills of negotiation, for example, the making of threats and promises, the use of persuasion, the signaling of concessions, and the development of compromises and creative solutions. As usual, the existence of cross-cultural differences complicates things further. Most international tourists know, for example, that there are some countries in which it is accepted custom to haggle in shops over the price of souvenirs, and others where one is expected to pay the marked price without any fuss.

NEGOTIATING STYLES

One way of understanding cultural differences is to divide up the typical negotiation into phases and to note that there are intercultural differences in the proportion of time or emphasis on each phase. The phases are:

- building a relationship
- exchanging information
- trying to persuade each other
- making concessions and reaching agreement[16]

Generally, people in Western cultures take a relatively "transactional" approach to negotiation, focusing mainly on the last two stages. Many other cultures pay more attention to creating a background relationship, which will make agreement more likely, that is, emphasizing the social side of the situation over the task side. The case of Bill Miller at the beginning of Chapter 1 is an example of people from two cultures not being able to negotiate with each other because each was stuck in a different part of the process. Culturally intelligent Americans learn to be sociable and patient in situations like that one, and culturally intelligent Asians and Latinos learn to get to the point a little more quickly.

Styles of persuasion may also differ. In political and business negotiating in Western societies, rational argument is favored, whereas in some other countries appeals to emotion or to ideology may be used. Again, Western negotiators, in line with their individualistic values, are relatively competitive in their negotiating style, seeing the situation as a win-lose situation and aggressively seeking the best deal they can get, if necessary by beating the other party. Asians are likely to be more polite, more obscure, and more restrained.

Another key cultural variable is power distance (see Chapter 2), the extent to which people expect to see power and authority invoked to solve problems. The arbitration model of negotiation supposes that whenever there are differences of interest to be negotiated, there should be a higher-level authority figure who can resolve any problem by making a decision that is imposed on all parties. This is often observed in Japan. Another model is the bureaucratic one, which attempts to reduce the need for negotiation by specifying in advance rules and procedures suitable for solving disagreements. This is often observed in Germany.

Collectivists prefer bargaining, mediation, and (as we have seen) creating relationships before getting down to serious negotiating, whereas individualists are happier in the competitive situation of preparing arguments and acting as an advocate. In cross-cultural negotiation it may be possible to use combinations of these different methods, but doing so requires all parties to step temporarily outside their normal conventions.

Again, there are differences in the details of negotiating, for example, the level at which initial offers are made, and the willingness of the negotiator to make concessions. An American negotiator might be put off by a Chinese, Arab, or Russian counterpart, because these groups seem to start off with extreme positions. Russians are also reluctant to make concessions, seeing this as a sign of weakness, whereas other groups such as North Americans and Arabs will make concessions and respond to others' concessions. To complicate matters further, negotiators alter their behavior when they are negotiating with people from different countries. Finally, of course, the generalizations made above about different cultural groups' negotiating styles are subject to substantial individual differences.

Principles for Cross-Cultural Communication and Negotiation

While there is plenty of information available on cross-cultural communication and negotiation, both from everyday observation and from systematic research, the picture it paints is so complex that it is difficult to spell out hard-and-fast rules for communicating and negotiating. However, here are some broad principles based on our model of cultural intelligence.

- *Gain the knowledge to anticipate differences.* Learn what you can of the codes and conventions of groups that you plan to deal with. Be aware of all the various areas of difference in communication we have noted in this chapter—for example, verbal versus nonverbal, contextual versus noncontextual, different negotiating styles. Learn the prevailing cultural values of the country—for example, individualist versus collectivist—and think about how these may influence the communication and negotiation process of your contacts.

- *Practice mindfulness.* Observe and pay attention to the *context* and the *conventions* of communication. There is a tendency to focus on the *code* and *content* of messages, but attending to *how* messages are delivered is, as we have seen, a way of acquiring much additional information. Additionally it is important to question attributions. In Chapter 3 we discussed the process in which we go behind surface behavior of others to attribute motivation and meaning. As we have seen, the meaning we usually attribute is based on a familiar understanding of our own behavior and that of our cultural group—for instance: "If I said or did that it would mean that I disagree, therefore when she does that it must be because she disagrees." Practicing mindfulness helps us to see new possibilities for the meaning in the behavior of other cultural groups.

- *Develop adaptive skills.* The question of whether and how much to adapt your behavior to accommodate the codes, conventions, and style of another culture in a negotiation situation is complex. The fact that you and the other party have potentially conflicting goals makes this situation the most challenging. Should you try to imitate them or just be yourself? Some degree of adaptation seems to improve relationships by making the other party more comfortable. However, too much adaptation can generate suspicion and distrust. Finding the optimal point of adaptation is more art than science. However, by practicing the steps outlined in this book for good cross-cultural communication and improving your cultural intelligence, you can gain a broad repertoire of adaptive skills and the knowledge of when they are appropriate.

Summary

Communication is fundamental to all social interactions and relationships, especially in business. Cross-cultural communication presents many possible barriers to shared understanding because individuals from different cultures don't share a common background, codes, or conventions. While language skills are important, cross-cultural communication involves much more than differences in languages. The culturally based codes and conventions of language also have to do with nonverbal signals and communication styles. Negotiation is a special communication situation in which the parties have potentially conflicting goals. While all negotiations follow a similar process, the emphasis placed on each stage of the process varies considerably across cultures. The challenging nature of negotiations makes high cultural intelligence a prerequisite for knowing when how and how much to adapt one's behavior to achieve the most successful outcome.

CHAPTER 7

Leadership Across Cultures

CLASS CONDUCT

Kenichi Tokuzawa, a Japanese man of twenty-four, was a university student of languages, and was fluent in a number of Western languages, including English. He was also a skilled teacher, because, prior to his university study, he had trained as a schoolteacher and had worked for two years in a Japanese primary school, teaching a range of subjects to ten-year-olds. Kenichi had been acclaimed as an outstanding young teacher and put his success down to his clear structuring of class objectives and syllabi, his meticulous preclass preparation, his articulate use of language, and his ability to make topics interesting for his students. The results were impressive: when Kenichi taught, every student paid close attention.

In his final year of language study, Kenichi, one of the best students in his group, won an international scholarship enabling him to spend a semester studying at a well-known university in New England. It was a most attractive opportunity, and, to put icing on Kenichi's cake, it included the opportunity to teach, part-time and on salary, at a local high school, where he would conduct daily classes in conversational Japanese with a tenth-grade class of American students.

Kenichi was excited at the opportunity to combine his teaching background with his knowledge of both Japanese and English. He realized it would be a challenge to teach students from another culture who were much older than those he had taught before, but he reasoned that his thorough preparation and proven teaching techniques could transcend cultural boundaries. He had heard that American students took a more relaxed approach to their study than did Japanese and expected to participate more in class, but as a younger Japanese well educated in U.S. culture, he thought he would be able to get on the same wavelength as American teenagers. As for class participation, that was essential in any form of language teaching, as students needed constantly to practice aloud the pronunciation of the new words they were learning.

On his first day in his new class, Kenichi, immaculately dressed, walked to the front of the classroom, bowed, smiled, and said, in excellent English, "Good morning. I am Mr. Tokuzawa. I am here to teach you Japanese." A few of the girls tittered, and several of the boys went on talking among themselves as if he had not spoken. A little rattled, Kenichi tapped the desk loudly with his pen. "Please listen to me," he said, more loudly, and repeated his greeting. This time there was more attention, but also further suppressed giggles. A youth at the back of the class, lounging in his chair, rolled his eyes toward the ceiling.

Kenichi realized there was a real possibility of a challenge to his authority, and decided to impose it. Briskly, he asked a student to distribute his meticulously prepared course notes. Clearly and methodically he explained the syllabus and grading system for the classes ahead. He asked if there were any questions. There were none. Rather than being eager to participate, the students seemed bored, listless. It was the same when he started teaching. He taught well, clearly, following exactly the carefully prepared schedule he had devised weeks before. He asked the students to repeat his words back and to translate, and a few did so. But it seemed that they did so unwillingly, as if they were answering his questions only to break the silence. The atmosphere at the front of the class was leaden. At the back of the class it was restless. The boy who had rolled his eyes put his head down on his desk and appeared to go to sleep.

Dismissing the students at the end of the class, Kenichi overheard a girl remark to her friend as they exited, "Is that guy uptight! He ought to chill out." "Chill out"? He wasn't sure he knew the expression. But he did realize that his first class had been a major step backwards. Whatever the reason, the class was just not in a mood to listen, to learn, to be led by him. Why? Were they just not interested in the subject? Were these simply the norms of the school, or the United States, in all classes? Or was there something he himself had simply got wrong?

In this case, the problem Kenichi faces is one of *leadership*. Leadership has been defined as "the ability to influence other people to strive willingly to reach common goals."[1] Kenichi is not just the teacher of the class, he is its leader. It is his job to get the class interested in the common goal of learning Japanese and influence them to "strive willingly" toward the goal.

Why has he not succeeded? While we do not know enough about the case to say for sure, it seems most likely that his style of leadership was too Japanese to achieve a good fit with the culture and expectations of his American students. Japanese have a higher level of power distance (see Chapter 2) than Americans; that is, they expect and accept that a leader will exercise authority as a right. Japanese show more respect to leaders because of their positions, whereas in the United States leaders have to earn respect through their actions. In Japan, respect is shown partly by *not* participating, that is, by respecting what the leader says and does and waiting until the leader asks you to make a contribution before speaking. Japanese schoolchildren are therefore much more respectful to their teachers than Americans are and much more ready to pay attention and accept the teacher's teaching without question. The Americans in Kenichi's class might have responded better if he had been less formal, and had found out more about them—by being mindful—before launching into his own agenda. Kenichi will have his work cut out for him if he is to get his students to be receptive. Can Kenichi lead this class? Is he a leader?

What Is a Leader?

The definition of leadership presented above—the ability to influence other people to strive willingly to reach common goals—highlights what leaders do. They influence others. However, when asked to think about leadership, most of us have an individual in mind who personifies leadership to us. The names of people often mentioned as great leaders range from Gandhi to Hitler, from Lee Ioccoca to Joan of Arc to Sun Tzu. The idea of great individuals is one that has had a great deal of influence on how we think about leadership. However, when we consider the leaders mentioned above, several questions arise, the answers to which can help us to become more culturally intelligent leaders.

- What made these people leaders and other people not?
- Would these people have been great leaders at another time, in another place, or indeed in another culture?
- Would these people have been great leaders with different followers, particularly followers who were culturally different from them?

The search for what makes a great leader first leads us to what might be called the "philosopher's stone" of leadership.

The "Philosopher's Stone" of Leadership

The philosopher's stone of history was a mythical chemical substance that reputedly had the property of changing base metals into gold, thereby making whoever discovered it rich beyond their wildest dreams. The philosopher's stone of management is leadership, the set of personality characteristics or practices, the universal "recipe" for leadership, that can change ordinary people into talented champions, each single-mindedly pursuing the organization's goals.

Unfortunately this "one best way" of leadership[2] is as mythical as the philosopher's stone. Different leaders influence their followers in different ways. A leader may capture the loyalty of some followers, while being rejected and ridiculed by others. A style that works perfectly in one situation (such as with construction workers in Dubai) may fall flat in another (such as with software engineers in Silicon Valley).

Even without taking the cultural dimension into account, leaders need to display the mindfulness-adaptability skills discussed in Chapter 3 just to understand the special features of the situation and vary their leadership to fit the amount of power at their disposal, the characteristics of their followers, and the tasks to be accomplished. Including cultural intelligence in leadership in addition to all these is a major challenge. Yet, as more and more leaders find themselves, like Kenichi Tokuzawa, dealing with followers who are culturally different (and, often, culturally diverse), in settings where different traditions and expectations for leadership exist, it is vital for any leader or prospective leader to develop a culturally intelligent approach.

Leadership Styles

Our understanding of culturally intelligent leadership begins with a look at leadership styles. Much of our understanding of how leadership works is based on research conducted in the United States that has then been assumed to be valid and has sometimes been applied around the world. These studies attempted to relate organizational performance—as indicated by measures such as productivity, quality, and staff morale—to different styles of leadership behavior. While researchers have used different ways of describing leadership styles, two dimensions that have shown up consistently are *concern for tasks* (getting things done, achieving organizational goals) and *concern for relationships* (getting on well with people, involving them participatively in decision making). Research indicates fairly conclusively and unsurprisingly that relationship-oriented leaders tend to have more satisfied subordinates, and that this is true across a range of different cultures.[3]

However, most business organizations are at least as interested in employees' performance as in their satisfaction, and the evidence on whether either relationship orientation or task orientation is related to performance is more complex. Task-oriented leadership, for example, can be demonstrated in different ways—by meticulous goal-directed planning, for instance, or by autocratic command. Moreover, people from different cultures react to task-oriented leadership in different and often unpredictable ways. There are also numerous other factors, such as the structure of the task, the power of the leader, and the behavior of subordinates—who, of course, are frequently trying to influence the leader just as he or she is trying to influence them—so that many possible propositions about leadership must be hedged with the proviso "it depends." In short, researchers are still a long way short of finding the leadership philosopher's stone that is applicable across all cultures. Consider the following examples of leadership around the world.

Leadership Around the World

THE ARAB WORLD

Leadership in Arab societies is a fascinating example of how history and culture can influence the traditions, practices, and expectations of leadership. Islamic religion and tribal traditions have always been strong and remain so, but Arabic countries are now touched by Western culture. Islam tends to make leadership a prerogative of males. Tribal traditions oblige business leaders to behave like fathers, protecting and nurturing employees as they would their children and taking responsibility for the whole business. Overlaying this system is the notion of bureaucracy historically introduced by the Ottoman

Empire and continued by Europeans in the twentieth century as a way of keeping control of their businesses.

The resultant leadership style has been termed "sheikhocracy."[4] It contains strong elements of personal autocracy and conformity to rules and regulations based on respect for those who made the rules rather than for their rationality. Rules thus have symbolic importance but will not be implemented if they go against autocratic-tribal traditions: for example, the bureaucracy may specify procedures for appointment on merit, but in the event these rules are likely to be ignored. Instead a leader will make appointments based on family relationships and friendships.

JAPAN

In Japan, one of the key factors that influence leadership is the cultural value of *amae*. *Amae* (somewhat loosely translated) means indulgent love, the kind that parents have for their children. In some societies, dependence on parents is socialized out of children at an early age, and they are taught to be independent and to stand on their own two feet. It is different in Japan, where *amae* is reinforced. All relationships in Japan, including manager-subordinate relationships, are affected by *amae*. It is therefore not surprising to find that Japanese managers take a deep interest in employees' personal lives. Subordinates often ask superiors' advice on all sorts of things including personal matters such as who would make a good spouse.

The existence of *amae* in Japanese relationships also gives rise to other cultural norms that influence leader behavior. *On* is a debt or obligation, and *giri* is the moral obligation to repay the debt. Leader behavior in Japan is embedded in a network of reciprocal obligations (*on* and *giri*) such that every action creates both a debt and an obligation to repay. A leader who neglects the obligation to reciprocate will lose the trust and support of subordinates. A Japanese leader's effectiveness is thus based, more than anything else, on the ability to understand and attract subordinates.[5]

THE OVERSEAS CHINESE

Ethnic Chinese living outside mainland China have a leadership style that reflects their modern organizations but is firmly entrenched in Chinese culture and tradition. In Chinese culture a leader's legitimacy is based on loyalty to the patriarch. Similarly, the word of the founder or CEO of modern Chinese organizations is law, and his authority resembles that of a head of the household more than that of a head of a business. All key people in the organization are related to the founder, and to each other, by blood or marriage. This authority structure allows the overseas Chinese to run their modern corporation as a family business. Mutual trust among family members— to base decisions on what is best for the clan—underlies all leader-follower relationships.[6]

FRANCE

Leadership in France is heavily influenced by the strong societal emphasis on hierarchy. At the top of French organizations is the CEO, who will have attended the "right" university, one of the Grande Écoles. The style of these top managers is often paternalistic and charismatic in the style of the great field marshals of France.[7] Between the top managers and the workers is a large group of middle managers or *cadres*, who deal with a plethora of rules and regulations. While seeming bewilderingly inefficient to the outsider, these organizations operate very reliably.

RUSSIA

The image of Russian leaders as powerful autocrats is based on the country's long history of centralized authority and responsibility.[8] In medieval Russia, village elders were entrusted to represent the common will of the people, and suggestions and criticisms were never attributable to any one individual. It was the elders' task to sort through the comments, and once they made their decisions, they went unchallenged and bore full responsibility for the welfare of the group. Later, under state socialism, these same traditional attitudes toward power and responsibility were evident in communist organizations. While advised by workers councils, the heads of these enterprises wielded all the power and also bore all the responsibility.

This centralization of power resulted in a top-heavy bureaucracy that some suggest was the fatal flaw in the socialist system. When things went wrong, as they often did, no one would take action without authorization from a superior. As Russian firms try to find their way in their new free-market environment, managers now struggle to push responsibility down the hierarchy and to delegate routine tasks. Consider the following case:

MBO IN RUSSIA

Dahl Ekelund, the newly appointed Norwegian executive director of the Russian subsidiary of Motor Corporation was conducting a seminar with his seventeen subordinate managers to introduce the concept of Management by Objectives (MBO).[9] Dahl had recently been appointed by the board of directors in the hope that his extensive track record as a leader in various European engineering enterprises would enable him to release some of the potential in a workforce that was well-qualified, talented, and experienced but knew little about market-based enterprise or modern management.

Dahl was amazed by the undisguised hostility directed not only at what he was saying but also at himself as the executive director. When he started to discuss the need for all employees to set their own written objectives, his subordinates actively came out against the proposal with comments such as: "We have lived without this kind of thing for five years and have made great strides. And we are still thriving. We don't need a new bureaucracy."

Dahl explained how MBO works, and how it provides new opportunities for staff involvement and participation at all levels. This brought the retort that he was not the first to try to implement Western managerial methods in the company—nobody had succeeded, and those who had tried were now working somewhere else.

Clearly irritated, Dahl answered brusquely, "Anybody working around me is going to be using these modern methods."

After this comment, you could have heard a pin drop.

In conclusion Dahl said that he expected a written outline of next year's goals from each of his subordinates within two weeks. He also asked them to get the same information from their own subordinates within three weeks.

As he left the room, Dahl overheard the following comments:

"Well, now, Petrovich, you'll be establishing goals rather than working. . . ."

"Not in my lifetime, let him do it himself. . . ."

"But, what about bonus? Didn't you hear, only those who reach the goals get the bonus."

"Yeah, we'll see."[10]

In the case above, the leadership expectations of the Russian subordinates are shaped by both Russian culture and years of living and working under state socialism. These Russian middle managers demonstrate an expectation for autocratic leadership and have great difficulty accepting, or trusting, their own participation or that of their subordinates in setting goals. Their reluctance is exacerbated by a healthy skepticism about the extent to which their superiors are concerned with, or capable of, controlling their futures, because under state socialism each autocratic boss was someone else's puppet.

In seeking to help the company move into a more market-oriented future, a higher CQ Dahl Ekelund might have applied cultural intelligence by:

- avoiding the *Be Like Me* approach to management that he had learned based on his cultural background in Western Europe (*knowledge*)

- taking more time to learn in detail some of the special characteristics of the new culture that he was entering (*knowledge*)
- spending time observing and talking to his new subordinates for a few weeks after arrival, trying to understand their collective and individual areas of comfort and discomfort before trying to institute change (*mindfulness*)
- trying to understand from the Russian perspective *why* they might be acting the way they were (*mindfulness*)
- listening to what his staff were saying (and being aware of what they were not saying) rather than becoming irritated and walking out of the meeting (*mindfulness* and *adaptive behavior*)
- introducing a less ambitious form of MBO, for example, one in which leaders helped set goals for their subordinates at first and then made a more gradual move toward participative methods (*adaptive behavior*)

These examples of leadership in Arab countries, China, Japan, France, and Russia show the complexity of the forces affecting leadership. Note the importance of historical factors, tradition rather than reason, and the acceptance, under the right circumstances, of apparently autocratic leadership. Managers with high cultural intelligence are mindfully attentive to such factors and work hard to develop even deeper knowledge. An international manager known to one of the authors, whose job took him into leadership roles all round the globe, would voraciously read books on the history and customs of the countries he was due to visit in order to acquire background knowledge and sensitivity to the local situation.

Culture and Expectations of Followers

As suggested above, another aspect of culturally intelligent leadership involves focusing not on the leader but on the followers. In some ways the idea of leadership is an invention of those who want to be in charge, or who believe that their traditional or hierarchical positions entitle them to be in charge. But in a sense, everyone is in charge; everyone has the potential to exercise leadership. We have defined leadership in terms of influence, and influence may be exercised by anyone, from the highest to the lowest member of an organization. Therefore, in understanding how leadership works across cultures we need to look at every participant—how they might understand a situation, whether they might expect a leader to decide for them what they should do, or whether and how they might seek to exercise influence in their own right.

The designated leader needs to think not just about how he or she might exercise influence but about how that influence might interact with the influence exercised by others to bring about a good result. For example, Dahl Ekelund, if he is smart, can set goals for his subordinates exactly as they want him to, yet still use the formal and informal processes that are part of their culture to find out their views and consider them before determining the goals.

To begin to understand the leadership expectations of different cultural groups, consider the key values dimensions outlined in Chapter 2.

- In *individualist* cultures people are concerned about themselves, prefer activities to be conducted privately, and expect decisions to be made by the individual according to his or her judgment and the anticipated rewards.

- In *collectivist* cultures people view themselves as members of groups and collectives, prefer group activities, and expect decisions to be made on a consensus or consultative basis, where the effects of the decision on everyone are taken into account.

It is evident that two very different styles of leadership would be expected in the two types of cultures. Western countries tend to be individualist, so both leaders and followers will attempt to involve themselves in decision making to maximize their individual influence and gain for themselves a good result. Higher management frequently tries to utilize individualism to advantage by offering the leader a high individual reward for the accomplishments of the group, or by holding the individual leader accountable for the performance of the group as a whole. Collectivist societies can rely more on the leader to involve the group, because that will be the shared expectation of both leader and group members.

Now consider some other key cultural values in terms of their likely effect on leadership:

- *Power distance*—The practice of autocratic leadership is more likely to be adopted and tolerated in a high power-distance culture, in which large differentials of power, for example, as between a boss and a subordinate, are expected and tolerated.

- *Uncertainty avoidance*—In cultures with high uncertainty avoidance, leaders who structure the work of their subordinates, possibly through bureaucracy, and who make decisions that enhance stability, will presumably do well.

- *Masculinity/femininity*—The relative emphasis on traditionally male goals of ambition and achievement and traditionally female orientations to nurturance and interpersonal harmony will influence leader perceptions. Leaders who nurture their relationships with group members while neglecting personal opportunities for recognition and promotion may be common in a feminine culture but may be considered eccentric in a masculine culture.

Other cultural forces influence expectations of leaders in similar ways. Some cultures value formality, and a leader will be expected to honor appropriate ceremonies and observances. In cultures where punctuality is important there will be pressure on leaders to turn up on time. In societies that focus on the future, a leader will be expected to focus on long-term strategy and to express that focus in his or her words. Because of the special status of the position, the leader is often the most led member of the group—led, that is, by the cultural milieu in which leadership is exercised, which in the end may be more powerful than the leader.

Cultural differences in expectations of leadership affect the perception of who is perceived as a leader. Different cultures have different prototypes of what a leader should be like. A leader who is able to meet followers' expectations of a good leader can expect to develop better trust and relationships with the group. In the following case, consider what was required of Ernesto in order to meet his followers' expectations of leadership.

MACHISMO!

Working in the banana plantations of Central America is difficult. The scorching sun and oppressive humidity make the ten-hour days seem endless. Pay is low and the food is terrible. Sanitation is inadequate; diarrhea is common. Yet the men who harvest the banana crop each cut tons of bananas every day.

Ernesto was a field foreman. His job was to make the men on his crew work hard—he pushed them to keep production high. To make money, labor costs had to be kept low and productivity high. Often men would gripe among themselves that Ernesto was too demanding.

One day, Manuel, a new, young, hardworking field hand, complained to Ernesto that he was pushing him too hard. The older workers looked on in silence. Ernesto told Manuel that if he wanted to keep his job he should do as he was told.

Later that day, Manuel again complained to Ernesto. Ernesto told Manuel that if he complained again he would be fired.

Manuel swung his machete at Ernesto. Instead of ducking, Ernesto blocked the blow with his hand. With blood gushing from a deep wound, Ernesto pinned Manuel to the ground. Two workers helped subdue and remove Manuel.

At his retirement party, twenty-one years later, Ernesto's longtime

> coforeman, Armando, recounted this story to the assembled friends. He told them—suppressing a tense laugh—that after that incident Ernesto's authority was never challenged.[11]

Thankfully, most of us will never have to demonstrate the kind of machismo that Ernesto did in order to be considered a leader by our subordinates. However, this case underscores the importance of having knowledge of the kind of leader behavior expected by subordinates and of making a mindful decision about what behavior from your repertoire to exhibit. In addition to highlighting the importance of the expectations that followers have of leaders, it also shows that leadership can accrue to people by other than formal means.

It has long been known that there is a difference between formal leadership (in which the leader is formally appointed and has an appropriate job title) and informal leadership (where someone has leadership status because of the respect of others). Informal leaders arise because their ideas (or behavior) are representative of others and because they practice good influence skills in putting these ideas across to others. Ideally, the formal and informal leaders are the same person, but often in a cross-cultural situation a formal leader from another culture may be poorly accepted because of cultural differences—particularly differences in expected methods of leadership—and there may be an informal leader from the home culture representing the ideas of the rank and file and exercising countervailing influence. This can make it important for formal leaders either to exercise a leadership style that fits in with local expectations or to be able to work with the informal leader.

The Common Thread: Charismatic or Transformational Leadership

An idea that has dominated thinking about leadership in recent decades is transformational leadership, which influences people to transcend their own immediate interests and objectives and to work hard to achieve not just desired performance, but performance beyond expectations.[12] To do this the leader has to present not just an immediate transactional reward for behavior but also a compelling vision of the future. The leader must aim not just to motivate members but also to inspire them, must demonstrate or model the behavior desired from followers, must stimulate and challenge followers, and must show individual consideration to each follower—considerations that are facilitated if the leader has the cultural knowledge and mindfulness characteristic of high CQ.

Perhaps the easiest way to understand transformational leadership is to return to the type of well-known leader such as Winston Churchill, John F. Kennedy, and Martin Luther King. However, Eastern leaders such as the Indian political and spiritual leader Mohandas Gandhi also meet the criteria for transformational leadership, as does the great South African leader Nelson Mandela, even though they may practice it in a very different and much lower-key way, and one that is in tune with the expectations and cultural values of their followers. Note the cultural variety of these exemplars. A leader with high cultural intelligence will be able to provide a vision, engage others' motivation, and model behavior in ways consistent with the culture and values of followers.

Indeed, there is research that supports the effectiveness of transformational leadership across a range of different countries.[13] Yet people from different countries have different ways of expecting leaders to act, even within a shared overall definition of transformational leadership, and there may be countries, such as Japan, where for a variety of cultural reasons its effectiveness is limited. In any case, it may be that the practice of transformational leadership requires special personal characteristics that may not be available in every leader. It is even more important to get the basics right in terms of understanding how to fit concern for task and concern for people within the specifics of the cultural setting.

Culturally Intelligent Leadership

Making sense of leadership is difficult enough, even without the complication of cultural differences. While there is no universally effective prescription for leading culturally diverse followers, there are some things we can say for certain that culturally intelligent leaders know and do.

- Leadership is largely in the minds of followers. If followers perceive a person as a leader, he or she will gain the power, authority, and respect afforded a leader.

- Some characteristics that followers look for in a leader are a) a vision for the group or organization, b) the ability to clearly communicate this vision to others, and c) skill in organizing followers toward that vision. However, the behavior that indicates these characteristics is different in different cultures.

- The leadership dimensions of task orientation and relationship orientation exist in every culture. Again, however, the behaviors that indicate a task orientation rather than a relationship orientation are specific to different cultures.

- Some followers need more leading along each of these dimensions than others. Factors such as organizational norms and the education levels of followers can act as substitutes for leadership. For example, a group of research scientists typically need very little in the way of task orientation from their leader. They already know what to do.

- Finally, trying to mimic the behavior of a leader belonging to the followers' culture is a double-edged sword. Some adoption of these behaviors will gain a leader acceptance by followers, but too much can be interpreted as insincere or even offensive.[14]

In summary, if you want to be a culturally intelligent leader, you will need to use knowledge and mindfulness to develop a repertoire of behaviors that can be adapted to each specific situation. Doing so involves knowledge of the likely expectations of followers in different cultures based on generalizations from cultural values like individualism and collectivism. Through mindful observation you will refine these expectations over time. However, you will also need knowledge of your own preferred style of leadership. What balance of task and relationship orientation feels normal to you? Will you have to work harder at being a relational leader if the situation calls for it?

You will also need knowledge of what organizational norms exist in your situation. Trying to be a participative boss in an organization that does not value participation can be counterproductive. Here, mindfulness also means paying attention to follower reactions to particular leadership behaviors and adjusting as necessary.

In cross-cultural situations, it is probably best not to model your leader behavior after a leader in the follower culture. In addition to looking silly trying to behave like Sun Tsu (if you are not Chinese), you may find that follower expectations of indigenous leaders may be very different from their expectations of you. Also, in multicultural groups followers can have very different expectations. Therefore, a better role model is a leader like you (from your own culture and so on) who has been particularly effective with these followers.

THE CULTURALLY INTELLIGENT "TERMINATOR"?

In October 2003, our attention was seized by an event of major cross-cultural significance in the United States—the election by the people of California of Arnold Schwarzenegger, a native Austrian with a thick European accent and a background in bodybuilding and acting, to the key leadership position of governor of the state.

Why did the American citizens of California make this choice? There are many answers, but one that stands out is that Schwarzenegger is a good cultural fit with the United States. In his personal demeanor and expressed values, and even more in the action-hero roles he typically plays in films, Schwarzenegger behaves very much in accord with American expectations of leaders. He is strong, decisive, powerful, active, and rebellious. America's two dominant cultural values are individualism and masculinity, and Schwarzenegger mirrors these unerringly. Is this a lucky match, or is the Terminator more culturally intelligent than we imagine?

As indicated in this case, the needs of followers are extremely important in determining their perceptions of leadership. In the end, however, a culturally intelligent leader is able to find a leadership style that strikes a balance between his or her preferred (normal) style, the expectations of followers, and the demands of the situation. This balance is always likely to be imperfect, a work in progress. As with surfing or skiing or riding a bike, this balance is initially very difficult but becomes easier and feels more natural over time.

Summary

In this chapter we introduced the problem of practicing culturally intelligent leadership. Influencing others toward goals is difficult in itself. However, when the dynamics of cross-cultural interactions are added, the challenge is even greater. Our understanding of leadership is greatly influenced by individuals we envision as great leaders, who share a similar ability to communicate a vision and to organize followers. In addition, the idea that leaders can exhibit a task or relationship leadership style has a universal appeal. However, the variety of behaviors that leaders around the world exhibit raises questions about any universal approach to leadership. This chapter suggests that understanding the expectations that followers have of their leaders is a key element in a culturally intelligent approach to leadership. This plus an individual's preferred style and the constraints imposed by the situation provide the three dimensions among which the culturally intelligent leader must find balance. While initially difficult to find, this balance become easier with each iteration of the knowledge, mindfulness, and behavioral skills process of cultural intelligence.

CHAPTER 8

Multicultural Teams

PARTICIPATE, AND THAT'S AN ORDER!

Harry is the leader of an advertising agency account team. The team's task is to develop advertising campaigns for a manufacturing company's range of power lawnmowers. The four members of the team are all from different cultural backgrounds. And they seem to be at odds with each other. Harry, an American, has strong ideas about what the campaign should be like; he talks about it a lot, and tries to persuade his three colleagues. But despite his strong views, Harry recognizes the value of diversity, of different ideas. He makes it clear to his colleagues that he *welcomes* alternative ideas. He would be delighted if someone were to come up with a campaign idea that was better than his. Harry says frequently, "Two heads are better than one, and four heads are better than two." His three team members eye each other cautiously.

So far the only person who has responded to Harry's invitation is Ingrid, a recent immigrant from Germany. And Ingrid has ideas about the lawnmower campaign that are not only different from Harry's but also diametrically opposed. Furthermore she has had twenty years' experience in the industry back in Germany and believes she has forgotten more about advertising than Harry has ever

142

learned. She is not about to back down on her ideas. She too talks, frequently and forcefully, about the new campaign. Harry doesn't agree with her, and argues back, loudly. But after all he did say he valued alternatives.

The other two members of the team keep a low profile. José, who is of Latin American background, can't stand Ingrid. How *dare* she talk to the boss like that! Has she no respect for authority? It's not so much that José doesn't agree with Ingrid's ideas—in fact secretly he thinks they are quite good—it's the rude and aggressive way she presents them that he objects to, her contemptuous way of treating Harry as if she were equal to him, if not higher. José would rather cut his arm off than encourage Ingrid by supporting her ideas. So he sides quietly with Harry and wishes Ingrid would go away.

As for Taiwanese Ming, she too keeps quiet. Harry says he wants her opinions and ideas, but she doesn't think he means it. If he does, why does he argue so aggressively with Ingrid? If you really want to hear what other people think, Ming believes, you should behave as if you respect them. Listening to Harry and Ingrid makes Ming sad. These people are talented but completely egocentric. Ming believes good decisions are made through patient reflection, the respectful exchange of ideas, and the protection of the harmony of the group that will, after all, have to work together to implement the final decision. She wishes she knew how to implement this method with Harry and Ingrid. In the meantime, she puts forward her views when Harry asks her, but so timidly that Harry wonders if Ming herself believes what she is saying.

The differences in the group can be explained largely by the cultural dimensions that we introduced in Chapter 2. Westerners such as Harry and Ingrid tend to be high on individualism and moderate on power distance. This means that they will expect to put forward their own views strongly in a group situation. Furthermore, they have been brought up and educated to be articulate and persuasive in the way they talk. They tend to believe in a kind of creative conflict in which ideas are pitted against each other until the best one wins. Maybe if

Harry and Ingrid stick to it long enough, one will eventually persuade the other. But unless they are able to separate the ideas from the person presenting them, the growing rivalry between the two may make it difficult for either to admit that the other is right.

As for the others, it appears that José has such a high level of power distance—and the associated expectation that the authority figure should make decisions—that he is unable to accept Ingrid's form of intervention. And Ming appears to be a collectivist who is a little lost in an individualists' world: she expects modest harmonious discussions in which the goals of the group as a whole take precedence over individuals' egos. In a group where Ingrid expects the right to challenge, José expects the imposition of authority, and Ming expects a long, courteous decision process without conflict, it seems unlikely that a creative discussion will ensue.

Each member of the group has much to offer. Each has technical expertise vital to the group's task. Harry and Ingrid are full of ideas and articulate in presenting them. Ming's ideals of team harmony and her respect for listening and José's recognition of the ultimate need for decisiveness by the leader and acceptance of decisions have much to offer the group.

Each explicitly adopts both the behavior and the norms implicit in his or her cultural background. They have brought to this new group their own culturally based ideas for how groups should function. There is little evidence of mindfulness in the way they interact with one another. In both action and in observation, they stick to culturally predetermined scripts.

In addition to the increasing cultural diversity of the workforce mentioned previously in this book, there is another, related pressure: an increasing emphasis, in the way business is organized, on *teams* (as distinct from individual workers). Because of the growing diversity of the workforce, such teams, even in one's home country, are becoming more and more multicultural. This shift presents a dual challenge: how to *con-*

tribute to a multicultural team and how to *manage* a multicultural team.

Once people are organized into teams and expected to work collaboratively for the common good, it becomes impossible for the manager to try to handle multiculturalism by dealing with each employee individually according to his or her own cultural needs. The manager now has to manage not only a set of culturally different individuals but a *process* involving different cultural responses.

In our opening case, for example, if Harry were more culturally intelligent he would understand the various actions and intentions of his team members and be able to react appropriately to each and to integrate them into an effective process. He would help the group itself to develop cultural intelligence. In order to do this he must understand how groups function differently than individuals. That is, in addition to cultural intelligence, he needs knowledge of group types, group tasks, group structure, and group processes.

You don't have to go overseas to experience multicultural teams firsthand. You almost certainly don't even have to go outside your own organization. Probably you don't have to go beyond your own immediate workgroup. Most of us have direct superiors, colleagues, or subordinates whose cultural backgrounds are different from our own.

Some of these will be new immigrants, still struggling to adapt to the host culture. Others will be the children and grandchildren of immigrants, fluent in their new language and skilled in the practices and norms of the host culture but perhaps still influenced by the cultural norms and values which are inherent in their background: for example, a Muslim woman in a European country who no longer wears the *hijab* (a scarf that covers the head, face, and neck), but still acts deferentially to her male colleagues and is unwilling to speak her mind freely;[1] or a courteous Chinese, unable fully to understand the boisterous mock aggression of his English colleagues to each other ("Why do they smile when calling each other insulting names?"); or a naturally ebullient American depressed by the long silences of her Asian colleagues and wondering how to create some sociability in such an earnest work environment. Workforces all round the world are becoming culturally more diverse, and the effect is felt at a local level.

This creates a challenge, beyond those already considered, for the development of cultural intelligence. The task of the manager of any workgroup becomes not just to practice cultural intelligence, but also *to engender cultural intelligence in all members of the team* in their everyday interactions with each other and their overall work for the organization. Managing cultural differences in workgroups is not just managing a set of one-to-one relationships between oneself and others from different cultures. It can often mean managing situations in which the cultural difference among those being managed is itself an issue, as in the case that opened this chapter.

How Groups Work

An important feature of how groups work is the difference between *task* and *process*.[2] In groups, task activities are those that are directed toward accomplishing the goal the group is trying to achieve. For example, "I'd like to tell you my plan for the advertising campaign"; "If we do it that way we will run over budget"; "That's a good suggestion." Process activities are directed at examining and improving the ways in which the group goes about this task, for example, "Suppose we go around the group seeing what each person thinks before we start arguing about things"; "I think Jane has something to say, but no one is listening to her"; "We're running short of time, we'd better have a vote now." Process activities need not be positive: "I'm irritated that even when I ask for your ideas you won't tell me what they are"; "I feel intimidated when you argue so loudly"; "in my country we show respect for other people."

Although it is right and proper that groups should spend

most of their time dealing with the task in hand, failure to attend to process is a frequent cause of group dysfunction. Groups often become ineffective because their process is overly autocratic, or torn apart by personal conflicts, or indecisive, and they have no way of examining what they are doing and changing it. The problem is increased when the processes are complicated by cultural differences.

In the case above, the successful conclusion of the group task is a joint problem-solving objective. This depends on effective integration of ideas among all members of the group. However, the group's problems are culturally determined process problems. The participants all have different models in their heads of how the group process should work, but—due in part to the leader's preoccupation with the task and his assumption that the process will look after itself—they have no way of bringing these ideas to the surface and resolving the process issues.

Cultural intelligence provides a means of dealing with group development and process issues that are caused or exacerbated by cultural differences. However, cultural intelligence may also help solve the process problems associated with any group. High cultural intelligence enables the observing and understanding of the different actions and intentions of group members. It acknowledges the cultural diversity of the group and the legitimacy of each member and his or her cultural background. Understanding how members see their roles in the group is likely to improve the quality of its interpersonal interactions. Combining this awareness with an initial focus on getting group processes clear before proceeding to the detail of the task, the team described above could break its impasse and move on to a united achievement of its goal.

Types of Workgroups

Groups are not all the same.[3] One group of workers may have relatively independent jobs but may be placed in the same workspace or have the same boss. We might call these groups crews. Another group of workers may collaborate closely with each other in a process in which the specialist knowledge of each member has to be closely integrated with that of the others. A good name for such groups is teams. A third group may be a temporary group expected to solve a specific problem or produce a report or design, and then disband. This third type of group is often called a task force.

These differences are important because they involve different ways of working together and therefore put more or less pressure on the cultural aspect of group functioning.

- In *crews*, group functioning is often predetermined by set procedures and technology, which override the need for high levels of cultural intelligence. For example, the actions of the flight-deck crew of an airliner are routine in such a way that members can rotate through different crews without the changes making much of a difference. High cultural intelligence and analysis of process would not seem a high priority in this case, except for cases of emergency, when the crew has to depart from their routine script.

- *Task forces* might benefit from higher cultural intelligence, but their interactions are oriented to specific project objectives and are temporary: effective intercultural interaction is necessary but not the building of long-term intercultural relationships.

- *Teams* do require highly developed trusting long-term interrelationships between team members, and cultural intelligence and the management of intercultural differences become critical.

By and large, the management of cultural differences is more important for teams than for task forces, and more important for task forces than for crews. Knowing when cultural intelligence matters most can help managers structure workgroups effectively and understand why cultural differences have a big effect in some organizational groups and not in others.

Virtual Multicultural Groups

A type of work group that is becoming increasingly important is the virtual team (or electronically mediated group) composed of people who do not meet face-to-face. Such groups are made possible by advances in information technology, including teleconferencing, videoconferencing, e-mail, collaborative software, and intranet-Internet systems. Globalization, plus the fact that the output of more and more teams is in the form of information or decisions rather than products or services, makes such teams ever more common. These groups may be geographically dispersed, with members located around the world. Groups like these solve some of the problems of face-to-face multicultural groups but create others.

In virtual teams many of the normal cues of interpersonal communication are reduced or removed, so cross-cultural differences, including language differences, are less noticeable. Yet because it may be harder to examine group processes and cultural differences, problems relating to cultural variables may be exacerbated. Some people feel uncomfortable using electronic forms of communication, particularly if the information being conveyed is complex, novel, or subtle. The development of trust is more difficult in situations in which individuals have to work with others whom they cannot see or hear directly, and groups therefore tend to go through their developmental stages more slowly.

These are not reasons for avoiding geographically dispersed multicultural groups—again, information technology bestows a great boon by allowing groups to interact across enormous distances. But managers of such groups must be even more patient than usual and must create opportunities to introduce the missing characteristics of normal group functioning to the team. The three keys to overcoming the difficulties of geographic dispersion (virtuality) are:

- developing a shared understanding among group members about goals and group processes
- using information technology to integrate member skills and abilities
- the development of trust among group members[4]

Group Process and Performance

In both face-to-face and virtual teams, group effectiveness is typically assessed by objective measures of group output, such as production, quality, sales, and so on. However, group morale and cohesiveness is also important, as it tends to ensure that performance is maintained over time. In assessing groups, therefore, wise group leaders consider not just immediate performance but also the processes that the group uses to do its work, as well as the satisfaction and development of group members as a result of the experience. The cultural dimension makes the task of facilitating an effective group process more challenging. Managers and group leaders can (and to some extent should) determine many of the factors that affect how groups function. For example, the surrounding organization strategy and structure and the group's objectives and resources are all controlled by management.

However, groups are more than just collections of individuals within an organization, and they form their own social processes. For example, groups can develop negative processes that undermine the potential of individual group members and reduce group effectiveness. Two common such processes are known as groupthink and social loafing.

- In *groupthink*[5] the group overemphasizes harmony and consensus by killing off dissent and creative alternatives. A famous historical example was the U.S.-supported Bay of Pigs invasion of Cuba in 1961, which was approved by President John F. Kennedy's inner group of advisers, who moved quickly to decide that an invasion would be the correct policy and then came to regard their own judgment as infallible, stifled debate, and questioned the loyalty of any who disagreed.

- In *social loafing* [6] individuals reduce their efforts to complete group tasks in the belief that others in the group will compensate to get the job done. In classic experiments on tug-of-war teams, for example, it was found that as more and more members were added to a team, the average exertion that members of the team applied to the rope decreased. [7] Anyone who has been involved in completing group projects will have noticed this phenomenon. There often seems to be at least one person who is not doing his or her part.

Individualists, interestingly, are likely to take a stand against groupthink but also more likely to take advantage of the group situation by social loafing. It is easy to see how cultural differences such as individualism-collectivism could work for or against such dysfunctional processes. [8]

On the other hand, some groups can through their own natural processes spontaneously create a dynamic of performance or innovation that external managers simply could not prearrange. In particular, in response to the feel-good aspect of working on an intrinsically interesting problem with others who are different (but complementary) in their skills and outlook, workers may experience a release of individual energy or creativity or ideas. It is often exciting to feel the stimulus to thinking that you get from someone different from you, who thinks and talks in a completely novel way. Different cultures increase the range of viewpoints and approaches available and are therefore a potential asset in many group situations. The trick is to create a process that encourages them and capitalizes on them to create this synergy.

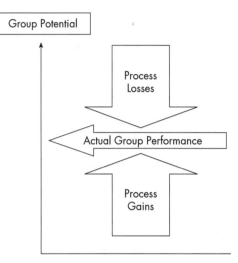

FIGURE 8.1. Effect of process on group performance

Thus we can talk about "process losses" of groupthink, social loafing, and so on, and "process gains" created from the range and diversity of alternative perspectives that are accrued from the diverse members and way the group goes about its business. The contribution of process to group effectiveness is shown in Figure 8.1.

A key task for the manager of a multicultural team is therefore to maximize process gains and minimize process losses. This task is about facilitating cultural synergy (getting the benefits of the cultural differences in the group) and overcoming destructive cultural conflict or difference. The culturally intelligent manager must consider three ways in which culture influences group processes. As mentioned previously, the first of these involves the cultural norms and scripts for how groups function that each member brings to a group. The other two are the amount of *cultural diversity* that exists in the group and the *cultural distance* among group members.[9]

Cultural Diversity in Groups

A group is diverse—or *heterogeneous*—to the extent that its members are different from each other rather than similar to each other. Culture is only one dimension on which work-group members are likely to differ; important others are gender, age, and experience. There is both good and bad news about the effect of diversity in workgroups.

The bad news about diversity is that research has shown that it tends to have a negative effect on the way people feel about the group.[10] For example, members of a diverse group are more likely to be dissatisfied with the group and less likely to identify with it, which can lead to serious process losses.

Sometimes managers respond to this kind of difficulty by making a deliberate policy decision to try to avoid multicultural groups as far as possible. This is one way of accounting for the worldwide phenomenon of countries taking in immigrants from culturally different overseas locations only to find that despite the immigrants' high qualifications, long experience, and strong work ethics, local companies simply prefer to employ less qualified local people. Low CQ local managers tend to think that if they employ immigrants they will suffer major process losses as the newcomers struggle to fit in. (In addition, of course, they may simply be prejudiced against them.)

AVOIDING DIVERSITY

To avoid process losses, some organizations have deliberate policies of making groups—particularly production groups—as homogeneous as possible. New Zealand, for example, has a high proportion of Samoan, Tongan, Cook Island, and other Pacific Island workers in the labor force of its cities. Some factories focus on a particular island community as the basis of their workforce or at least try to ensure that particular work teams or departments are made up of all Samoans or all Tongans. Although proponents of equal employment opportunity may not like such practices, managers will claim that they ensure there is no ethnic conflict and that each em-

> ployee feels comfortable with his or her "mates." One Auckland businessman occasionally flies his all-Samoan workforce to Samoa at his own expense for a "family holiday," and his business is cited as a model of good employment.[11]

The approach taken in this case is understandable, but it represents a short-term view. Process losses tend to be immediate, whereas process gains take longer to show up. Effort and sensitivity shown in welcoming and orienting people who are different is likely to be rewarded later on, when the process losses disappear and process gains kick in.

This is the good-news side of the argument about diversity in work groups. The same research that shows that diversity has a negative impact on job satisfaction and identification also shows that diversity, at least in task-related skills, tends to be positively related to group performance in organizational settings.

This finding may be understood by considering what is likely to happen in a totally homogeneous group—that is, a group totally lacking in diversity, a group where members are all similar. For example, consider a task force trying to find the solution to a technical problem. They are all German. They are all male. They are all graduate engineers. They are all in their fifties. They all studied engineering at the same university, and they are all long-service employees in the chemical engineering department of the same company. You will probably agree that, competent as they may be, they are unlikely to come up with a range of different ideas relevant to the problem.

Diversity typically provides groups with a wider range of ideas and viewpoints. Like all forms of diversity, diversity in culture encourages diversity in ideas. Culturally different people have different worldviews. And the wider the range of ideas, the better the chance of finding good ones. Research shows that that cultural diversity often results in more creative and higher-quality group decisions. This comes about not only because diversity means that more alternative viewpoints will be put forward, but also because being conscious of cultural difference in the group focuses the group's attention on process issues, including listening to minority viewpoints.[12]

In addition, being culturally different might relate directly to the group task. In an increasingly globalized world, culturally different group members may be selected for groups precisely because of the unique knowledge they have about culturally different environments. For example, Brazilian or Indian members might be recruited to advise a European or Chinese company planning to export to their countries, providing information about the cultural or local-market features of Brazil or India that may affect the campaign.

Cultural Distance in Groups

Another important factor in diverse groups is the *relative cultural distance* of group members. Cultural distance refers to how different each group member feels from each other group member.[13] For example, an Indonesian in a group with an American, a Canadian, and an Australian would feel much more distant from the group members than they do from each other. When we are very different from other people in a group it is noticeable to them and to us.

People who are somewhat culturally different from others in the group find it easier to become involved in group activities than those who are culturally *very* different. People are often aware of the great effort involved in overcoming extreme cultural differences. Rather than trying to cross what may be seen as an unbridgeable gap, they may prefer to withdraw from the group and keep their views to themselves. This happened to José in our opening case, in which the group was dominated by two westerners. If members withdraw, as José and Ming did, their potential to assist the group is wasted. Group leaders need to decide how to respond to such a situation: for example, should they transfer a culturally distant person to another group where she or he will feel more at home, or should they focus group energy on bridging the cultural gap?

Summarizing research findings about diversity in teams, we can say that diversity provides a team with greater potential for excellence than does homogeneity. But because of the process-loss phenomenon, the risks are also higher that the group will founder.

Culturally Intelligent Team Management

The existence of diversity in a group does not guarantee the kind of creativity suggested above; it merely makes it possible. The task of the manager or group leader is to facilitate a process that will allow the creative side of diversity to flourish. There are three things that culturally intelligent people can do to reduce or eliminate process losses and to capitalize on diversity. These are to manage the environment of the group, to allow culturally diverse groups to develop, and to foster cultural intelligence in the group.

MANAGING THE GROUP ENVIRONMENT

The functioning of any group also depends on the managerial environment—management support, rewards, group status, and opportunities for self-management—within which it functions.

Management Support. Any group requires good management support, in the form of such things as material resources, relevant information, and psychological support shown as goodwill and respect. Cross-cultural groups especially need to work in an organization where management respects cultural difference and appreciates the potential that diversity creates to improve the organization's creativity and performance. A culturally intelligent team leader attempting to capitalize on cultural diversity in the way we have described is likely to fail if external management (particularly senior management) is seen to operate in a different way.

Rewards. Individualists like to be rewarded on the basis of their own contributions. In other words, they believe rewards should be equitable. Collectivists like to be rewarded on the basis of equal shares for all contributing to the group; they believe rewards should be equal. This sounds like an impossible problem for those who have to decide how rewards should be allocated to members of a multicultural group. Devising individualized pay-systems rewarding each according to preference is impractical. And culturally diverse groups may develop their own consensus about an appropriate balance of individual and group rewards. However, virtually all of the research on this topic suggests that high-performing groups in any culture derive a substantial proportion of their rewards from group activities.[14]

Group Status. Most managers understand that, regardless of cultural composition, a group's high status in an organization will increase members' self-esteem. However, the extent to which this is true is also dependent on cultural differences: it is a matter of the place of the group in the individual's life. In some (primarily collectivist) cultures, it is a family group that is important to the individual above all others, so the workgroup is of much less importance. People in these cultures may care little about the status of the work group.

Self-management. Providing objectives or general direction for groups—especially for teams—and allowing them to self-manage by finding their own processes for reaching their objectives is an option for the managers of any organization. It is an option that is increasingly fashionable, for example, in the trend toward outsourcing and contracting. Research suggests that self-management has advantages for many teams, cross-cultural or not. For cross-cultural teams, it has the additional advantage of enabling team leaders to develop unique group processes for overcoming the specific cross-cultural issues of the team, without the likelihood of interference from the outside.

DEVELOPMENT OF CULTURALLY DIVERSE GROUPS

A key element of group development is the selection and allocation of members. As a manager you probably have some discretion—moderated perhaps by legislation or local policies pertaining to equal employment opportunity—to encourage or discourage diversity as you hire new staff and/or allocate staff members to particular groups. Such decisions need to be the products of careful consideration of issues covered earlier in this book. For example, are you prepared to accept and manage the likely short-term process losses of greater diversity, in order to benefit the prospective longer-term process gains?

Groups do not begin to function instantaneously. Their development can take place over an extended time. Four distinctive phases of group development have been identified. These are labeled *forming, storming, norming,* and *performing*,[15] in which the group members:

- first become familiar with each other (*forming*)
- go through inevitable conflicts that arise about who is doing what and how to go about things (*storming*)
- start to develop common expectations of each other (*norming*)
- finally work cohesively and effectively together (*performing*)

This process is likely to take longer in multicultural groups because of the greater differences in expectations about how groups should work. If you manage a multicultural group you may therefore have to be more patient in the way that you bring that group up to speed or integrate new culturally different members into the group.

Of course, one option is simply to wait for the group to develop on its own. Research shows that newly formed culturally diverse groups reduce their process losses over time by finding ways of working together better. However, in today's fast-paced business world, waiting for group development to occur on its own is probably not good enough. Culturally diverse groups often need feedback about the effectiveness of the processes they are using. In many cases this feedback is best presented from outside the group. Cultural intelligence helps managers strike the right balance between delegation and direction.

DEVELOPING CULTURAL INTELLIGENCE IN THE GROUP

The best way to capitalize on cultural diversity in groups is to ensure that group members have high CQ and group leaders have the will and the skills to explore process issues within the group. To facilitate the development of CQ, training of group members in cross-cultural understanding and skills is valuable.

All group members can benefit from understanding the concepts presented in this book. Also, encouraging each member to talk either in formal meetings or in day-to-day conversation about his or her cultural background and its effects is good. A colleague of ours calls this process of understanding the similarities and differences among group members "mapping."[16] Of course care must be taken to avoid making comments that are judgmental. Using this book by working through cultural issues on a chapter-by-chapter basis or encouraging members to consider whether they can identify with characters in any of the case studies may also be a source of productive discussion.

The key element in exploring process issues is the provision of feedback to group members, both from each other and from observers outside the group. By coming to a good understanding of the dynamics within the group and the causes of its difficulties, group members can develop new productive ways of changing both their scripts for the group and their own behavior in it.

Making Multicultural Workgroups Effective

It is clear that the existence and extent of multicultural work groups in any organization depends on factors external to the manager: for example, the composition of the available labor force, the hiring and firing policies of the organization, and top management support for diversity.

However, most people who have to lead and supervise multicultural groups have little influence over these matters and have to accept each situation as they find it and do their best to make it productive. Many situations may be multicultural, but every situation is unique. This means managers require not just CQ, but also the knowledge and ability to perceive and take account of the specifics of the group situation. For example, it is vital for the manager to figure out

- whether the group is a team, a task force, or a crew
- whether the team faces relatively routine or relatively complex tasks
- the degree of cultural diversity in the group, the specific cultural issues, and whether the group has come to terms with these issues
- whether the group has a natural process for surfacing and dealing with cross-cultural issues and for ensuring that all group members contribute, regardless of their cultural origins

Our analysis suggests that there may well be some culturally diverse groups that, because of the nature of their task or because they have found their own ways of functioning effectively, require little deliberate action to stimulate their cross-cultural understanding.

However, there will be other groups, particularly teams and perhaps task forces, that require interpersonal sensitivity and working closely together on complex tasks. Here, the leader/ manager must be proactive in assisting the group to examine, confront, and improve its own processes. Cultural scripts can be so diverse and so embedded in team members that resolution requires a major effort. However, the development of cultural intelligence in the team leader and team members can create a basis for mutual understanding and respect that will enable people to find their own ways to solve problems. Also, whatever the cultural mix, many of the techniques involved are in any case part and parcel of effective group leadership. In multicultural groups, the combination of CQ and team process skills can be a winning combination.

Summary

Groups are in fashion. The popularity of team-based work environments coupled with increasingly multicultural work forces makes the ability to get the most from culturally diverse work teams an important current issue. In order to effectively manage or participate in multicultural workgroups and teams, individuals need cultural knowledge but also knowledge of group types, group tasks, and group structure and processes. In order for these workgroups to function effectively, the group itself must develop cultural intelligence. Culturally diverse groups have the potential both for higher achievement and greater failure than single-culture groups. The trick that they must perform is to maximize the positive effects of cultural diversity while at the same time minimizing its negative effects. This goal is achievable by high-CQ leaders who also use group-process knowledge, practice mindfulness in group interactions, adapt behavior to accommodate the unique circumstances of the group, and encourage and train members to become culturally intelligent as well.

CHAPTER 9

Managing
International Careers

As John Northcroft walked through the Sydney airport toward the flights to Los Angeles and then Houston, he was reminded how familiar Sydney had seemed when he first went there. There had been nothing to indicate that he was in a foreign country. Although the accents were different, everyone spoke English, and Sydney was a big modern city with all the amenities of the United States. The only apparent difference was the reversal of the seasons. The hot and humid July he would see in Houston was very different from the mid-winter climate he was leaving behind. "That should have been a clue as to how different things really are," he thought.

John had been encouraged to take the post of MIS Manager for Med-Products Australia Ltd.—a subsidiary of Houston-based Med-Products International—to improve his chances for promotion back home. He had applied even though his wife and two teenage children were unenthusiastic about the move. And it *had* been tough on them. Finding a house similar to their Houston home had been difficult, and getting the children enrolled in the best schools had required meetings with school principals to sort out equivalent grade levels, requiring much of John's time. It wasn't long before the whole family was questioning the decision to move.

Colleagues at Med-Products Australia had organized a welcome party for the family soon after their arrival, and his wife had subsequently been invited out to lunch and the theater. However, the family had not been able to develop the kind of social network they had been accustomed to back in Houston. His family members missed their life in the United States. And, once, his son had asked if he could go back home to live with his grandmother. It was true, though, that John had been invited out several times for Friday after-work drinks with his employees. He hadn't attended any of these gatherings, however, because he wanted to spend any free time he had helping his family settle in.

John was confident that he could bring the efficient methods he had helped to develop in MIS in Med-Products' Houston headquarters to the Australian operation. Over the past eight months he had studied the MIS operations in Sydney and compared them to those he had developed in Houston. It was obvious to him that the Sydney operation was plagued by inefficiency, in part because of the flat organizational structure. He often found himself responding to requests and receiving information from technicians and supervisors as well as from managers and heads of department. The casual informal culture was also a problem. Compared to Americans he found the Australians less sophisticated, less organized, more egalitarian, less willing to defer to authority. They used an expression "she'll be right," meaning that, in the end, problems would sort themselves out. People seemed to hope for the best when instead they should be taking action! That was much too fatalistic an approach for the goal-directed Texan boss.

At a recent staff meeting he had outlined his plan to improve the Australian operations. This included a reduction of the number of managers reporting directly to John and encouraged specialization among the department's employees. It also included sharper systems of job description, accountability, and performance evaluation. It would make the Australian operation much more like the Houston one of which he was so proud.

At the meeting, John made a strong, carefully prepared presentation in support of his plan. He passed out copies of it and spent the next twenty minutes explaining his rationale. He explained that the plan was still in the draft stage and that he welcomed comments and reactions. After a few minutes of uncomfortable silence, he said,

"I'm sure you will want to give this plan some thought. Why don't you take a couple of days to look at it and e-mail any suggestions."

It was only a few days later that he heard from his boss back in Houston that a number of his Australian staff were seeking jobs elsewhere. John was astonished. He had always prided himself on his ability to recognize dissatisfaction among his employees. Now, he was being called back to Houston to discuss what was going on. He really didn't know what he was going to say.[1]

So far in this book, we have dealt with the immediate, micro-level effects of operating in a different culture. We have focused on the qualities of knowledge, mindfulness, and culturally intelligent behavior that help you to gain the cultural intelligence to operate in other countries and cultures. And we have focused mainly on work-related behavior. In this vein, we might say that John's problems with his staff were most likely caused in part by a kind of cultural imperialism—his unthinking imposition of his home culture, organizational and national—in an environment where it didn't really fit. But the problems were compounded by John's broader problem of integration into the new society, particularly his role as husband and father as he struggled to help his family to adjust.

The case presents us with a paradox of cultural intelligence—a paradox that it shares with many other areas of human development. The paradox is this:

In order to acquire cultural intelligence you must practice, by living and working in culturally different environments, or at least by working with culturally different people.

But

In order to live and work effectively in culturally different environments, or at least to work successfully with culturally different people, you first need to acquire cultural intelligence.

This problem is a difficult one. In practice, it means that John and people like him must do two things at once: observe and learn cultural intelligence on an ongoing basis at the same time as they do their day-to-day work. It seems John focused just a little too intently on his MIS mission and was understandably distracted by his family's adjustment problems. Had he adjusted more to the Australian culture he encountered, opening up, for example, to the "Aussie way" and trying little experiments in egalitarianism and informality, perhaps he would have been rewarded by improved performance and acceptance in his company, and he might have avoided the unwanted career interruption of his peremptory recall to Houston.

The case also reminds us that cultural intelligence is not just a party trick to be pulled out from time to time as intercultural situations crop up in work. Many managers' work necessitates the constant exercise of CQ. If you work in international business you may well find that it will eventually require you to uproot yourself and go overseas not just to negotiate and sell and lead in a different environment, but to live there. You may take your partner and family as well, giving you responsibility for their welfare as well as your own. Possibly you will live abroad for many years. Possibly you will travel frequently from your new home to other locations. Possibly you will move on eventually to third, fourth, and subsequent locations. Each move will involve simultaneously changing country, culture, job, home, and social contacts. Most moves will involve all those changes for a whole family. An international career may be necessary and can have huge benefits for the development of your cultural intelligence, which for some expatriates becomes a way of life, as natural as breathing. But such a way of life also creates complex problems of adjustment, which can be very stressful.

Expatriate Assignments

A common international career move is the *expatriate assignment*.[2] Expatriate assignments typically arise because an organization, usually a multinational company, wishes to keep control of its overseas interests in the hands of managers who are from the country in which the organization is based and who have critical technical expertise or a good understanding of the company's philosophy, strategy, products, and procedures. However, organizations vary in this respect, and some will seek to employ more locals than expatriates in management positions. A common pattern is to appoint many expatriates in management positions in the early stages of the development of business in an overseas location, then to pull them back gradually as local people learn the ropes. If you wish to pursue (or to avoid) international experience, you should evaluate what your employer's and any prospective employers' policies are with regard to the staffing of overseas operations.

In most expatriate assignments, the organization assigns an employee to a position overseas for a period ranging from a year to five years. Typically the organization identifies which of its current managers has the expertise needed, and offers him or her the opportunity of the overseas posting. But often people are chosen largely on the basis of relevant technical expertise: other criteria, including cultural intelligence, may be neglected. Individuals offered postings often accept them based on perceived career opportunities and financial rewards, without giving enough consideration to whether they are well enough prepared—particularly in terms of CQ—for such a major change and whether it will really be to their benefit in the long term.

Despite the recent progress of women in acquiring more and more positions on company ladders, more than 85 percent of expatriate assignees are male. This statistic may reflect age-old tribal patterns in which the men went far afield to hunt or gather, while the women stayed behind to keep the home fires burning. However, the tradition does not make good sense in today's world. While in some societies women face prejudice and exclusion from managerial roles, they also tend to have better interpersonal skills than men, and may have the potential to develop a higher CQ. There is a strong case to be made

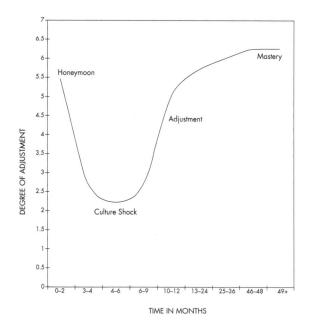

FIGURE 9.1. The U-curve of cross-cultural adjustment.

for organizations worldwide increasing the availability of overseas work for women.

Both organizations and individuals frequently predicate the move to an overseas location on the assumption that the individual will serve out the full intended term of the assignment and will then return to a superior position in the company back in the home country, where the additional knowledge gained overseas will have value.

In practice, many expatriate assignees return early from their assignments for various reasons—an event that is usually regarded as failure by the employing company. This premature return home is often the result of the expatriate's or his family's failure to adjust to the new culture.

Figure 9.1 shows a model of the phases that some experts believe expatriates go through.[3] The process follows a U-shaped curve through a honeymoon period, culture shock, attempted adjustment, and then mastery. In the honeymoon stage everything is new and exciting, as it would be to a short-term tourist. In the culture-shock stage, the differences between what the expatriate is used to and what the new culture provides become apparent, as the individual either learns—including developing his or her CQ—or cannot learn how to adapt. Those who get into the routines and rhythms of daily life in the new country move eventually to a position of mastery, while others may never properly adjust.

A real possibility for some people is that the adjustment is so successful and their view of the new country so positive that they lose all desire to return home. Others meet romantic partners in the new environment, and the couple must make the tough decision about which of them will make the other's country home. In these circumstances the expatriate becomes a migrant, and the career becomes truly international.

GOING NATIVE

As he looked out from the top-floor restaurant over Lake Michigan and the magnificent Chicago skyline, Yukimichi (Mike) Kusumoto thought about how his expatriate assignment to the United States had turned into a permanent move. Like many Japanese, initially he had had great difficulty adjusting to the extreme foreignness of the U.S. The crime-rate statistics were so frightening that he came to Chicago without his wife, Naoko, and family, intending to accomplish his assignment and then return to his firm back in Japan. However, what was even more frightening when he arrived was the amazing diversity in America. The sheer variety of people and cultures in Chicago was startling. And, at the office, he had initially been frustrated by the short-sightedness of his colleagues, their failure to treat customers as honored guests, and their use of lawyers to protect themselves from their own hasty decisions. Yes, adjusting to the United States had been very difficult.[4]

He couldn't say exactly when he began to feel more comfortable in Chicago than back in Tokyo. Of course his English was now very good, and Naoko had joined him after a year and had eventually integrated well into American society. By carefully observing and trying to understand American business practices, he had finally been very successful at work—so successful that a competing American company had eventually recruited him at a much higher salary. Even though he had insisted that his two daughters go to the special Japanese school in the Chicago suburb where they lived, they were now as American as they were Japanese—not a bad thing, he thought. Now he expected that they would attend an American university rather than go back to Japan. For himself, Yukimichi had grown to appreciate the American way of life. He enjoyed its freedoms and spontaneity and loved his spacious home and beautiful neighborhood—such a contrast with the tiny apartment he had left in Tokyo. He had even found himself admiring the independence of Americans, and he did his best to act that way himself. It seemed to suit his personality. Go back to Japan? No, he was an American now.

Who succeeds on overseas assignments, and who fails? Can you predict your likelihood of success? Thanks to decades of research on expatriate assignments, we have some answers (though they are limited by the fact that almost all the research has been carried out using samples of U.S. expatriates). Older expatriates seem to develop better commitment and adjustment than younger. Married expatriates perform better and are more satisfied than single.

The research also suggests that the better the adjustment of the spouse of the assignee, the better the adjustment and commitment of the assignee. Indeed, there are suggestions that family situation is the most critical factor of all in determining success. Some companies considering placing an employee abroad even interview the spouse as well as the employee.

Cultural intelligence may be important for the whole family. If you want your children to grow up with a high CQ in a world that will increasingly value it, why not give them a taste of international experience while they are still young and flexible enough to make the most of it? Like John Northcroft's children, they will need support and guidance, but it will be a great opportunity—gaining cultural intelligence as a family experience.

While personality tests fail to distinguish definitively between successful and unsuccessful expatriates, some new evidence suggests that the characteristics associated with cultural intelligence support effective adjustment.[5] Expatriates themselves state that the abilities to communicate, to establish relationships, and to handle stress are critical to their success. The ability to speak the language of the host country is also important but mainly as an expression of the willingness to communicate across cultures.

An organization can assist adjustment to overseas postings by providing appropriate training. Consistent with formal means of developing cultural intelligence (see Chapter 4), there is evidence that cross-cultural training assists expatriate adjustment, relationships with host nationals, and the overall performance of the expatriate. However, many firms believe cross-cultural training is not effective and do not provide it. If you have been given this book by your company as part of an education program for potential expatriates or for company members generally, that is a sign that the company is giving some thought to these important issues.

However, as we indicated previously, much depends on the quality and type of the training. For example, if the cultural distance of the other country involved is small, then a course supplying factual information may suffice. For larger cultural distances, where the demands on the expatriate are greater, it may be that longer, more experiential training is needed.

As the previous discussion suggests, in expatriate assignments the company becomes a more important part of the employee's life. Expatriates expect assistance with relocation, housing, family settlement, insurance, tax preparation, and many other things. Firms have high expectations about the performance of these very costly employees. However, the nature of careers is changing, making traditional expatriate assignments only one of many types of international career moves that you may consider.

The Changing Nature of Careers

Thirty or forty years ago, business companies tended to be large, stable, and bureaucratic. Managers were encouraged to think in terms of an organizational career, in which they made a long-term commitment to a single company. Their loyalty was typically rewarded by a company commitment to their job security and the likelihood of steady advancement up that company's career ladder.

Under the greater competitive pressures of recent years, many of those who had thought their jobs were safe were laid off. People began to see that they could no longer rely on the security promised to them by their employers. They became less committed to their current employers and more mobile.

These changes have caused employers and employees to shift their emphasis from building *long-term relationships* to negotiating *short-term transactions* in which the parties are in fact trading immediate benefits rather than thinking about abstractions such as loyalty, commitment, and career. This is important in the context of expatriate assignments. Are these assignments short-term transactions or building blocks in a long-term relationship? Employees are often suspicious—sometimes justifiably—that an employer may imply that the assignment is part of a well-thought-through relationship but may actually have no plan for developing the relationship or the employee further once the assignment is over. The employer likewise may worry that the employee will take advantage of the assignment by "jumping ship" and going to work for another company or even deciding to remain overseas forever. Expatriate assignments are further complicated by cultural differences. Those from individualistic cultures tend to view assignments as short-term transactions, whereas those from collectivist cultures see them as longer-term relationships.[6]

This shift in employer-employee relationships often makes the idea of taking an expatriate assignment with the promise of a promotion upon return less appealing than it might have been a few years ago. Additionally, the increased number of dual-career couples means that a significant career sacrifice on the part of one partner is often required in order for the other to accept a traditional expatriate assignment. All this means that expatriate assignments are not for everyone, and many people will have to develop cultural intelligence in other ways. Consider the following case.

DOING IT HER WAY

Margaret is English. She always had a taste for travel. At nineteen, she went traveling for two years in Europe, spending time particularly in Greece and Ireland. She funded her travel mainly by working as a bartender and in Greece even gained supervisory experience as a restaurant manager. Her experience in Greece sparked an interest in history, and she has always had a long-term orientation to business. So on her return to the UK she went to university to study history and economics.

By the time she finished the degree, however, Margaret had decided that she wanted a career in teaching. And she was also restless. She wanted to go traveling again first, perhaps to Asia this time. So she applied for, and gained, a place with JET (Japanese Exchange Teaching)—teaching English to adults in Japan. She considered that the opportunity would be culturally valuable to her and would enable her to try teaching and to save money. Her plan was to see as much as possible of Asia, learn to speak Japanese, develop some teaching skills, and save a nest egg to take home. Her assignment was in Osaka, with a contract for either one or two years.

Margaret soon settled into the JET work in Osaka. JET had rules stipulating that its employees were not permitted to take other work.

However, Margaret was soon approached by a local government organization wanting to hire her to set up a part-time English-language school. She thought this opportunity would enable her to gain further personal and professional development. JET turned a blind eye. The part-time work lasted six months, and the evening teaching it involved was interesting, as the students were keen to learn English. Also, the cost of living was such that she needed the additional income in order to earn her nest-egg. And it put her into a friendly social circle and enabled her to take trips and see Japan with the adult students.

Margaret had enough money and time away from teaching to do about three months' touring per year in Asia. She traveled with an American boyfriend, who was a colleague on the JET program. Other social contacts were Mama-san and Papa-san—a café-owner couple with whom she boarded. They adopted her, almost as if she were their own daughter. They showed her around, taught her about Japanese ways, communicated with her only in Japanese, and gave her part-time work in the café. Margaret's cultural learning was dramatic.

After two years, Margaret was offered an extension of her JET contract, but she wanted to return to Britain. She knew she wanted to live there, she wanted to see her parents and brothers again, and she wanted to own her own home. She had broken off her relationship with her American boyfriend.

She still would have liked to teach. But she thought about the negative attitudes of British school students as she had experienced them when younger and compared them unfavorably to those of the Japanese people she had been teaching. The mature Japanese were so polite and motivated compared with British pupils. She realized how poorly paid teachers were. She returned to the UK with some money but no real plan apart from a vague desire to get into management. She bought a small house in her home city.

She got a job as a sales rep for a company selling print and data-base solutions and soon realized that she had found her forte—selling. Then she was approached by her present employer, a software company, and took a sales job with them. The job is good but doesn't take all her energy or fulfill all her interests. She aspires to be a manager, or, better still, would like to start her own business. She learned a thing or two from Mama-san and Papa-san and the way they had turned their Osaka cafe into a gold mine! But she felt she lacked skills and knowledge relating to the wider business world and enrolled for a master's degree in business. She has a business plan—to start an export-based Internet company, selling British products overseas. For this venture, she sees Japan as a key market, and believes her understanding of the language and culture will assist her greatly.

Among the things Margaret learned overseas were language, patience, and what she calls "cultural sensitivity"—particularly how to interact with Asians (which she uses a lot in her current employment, where several of the staff are Indian or Chinese). She has a heightened awareness of the importance of education, plenty of self-confidence, a broader perspective. She also increased her drive: "It (the overseas experience) got me growing again—I caught up with my friends." She enhanced her cooking skills, her ability to speak in public, even her abilities in tennis and other sports. She learned judo.

Margaret considers that the most significant learning she did was about herself—who she was, what her skills were, what she wanted to do. But the appreciation of Japanese and Asian culture and its contrasts with Europe were also very important. Overall, Margaret says her time in Japan was "the best time of my life."

In her determined internationalism, Margaret is typical of many of today's young people. Two generations ago, most people tended to build their careers in their own neighborhoods. A generation ago they thought more broadly, in terms of anywhere within their own countries. Nowadays, many want to see the world. And many of them also realize that they cannot afford to do all the traveling they want as tourists, and that even if they could, being a tourist is often an experience that protects the individual from full contact with other cultures and could thus limit the development of CQ. Employment in another culture forces the employee to get to grips with it. So, increasingly, people work as they travel, and the acquisition of cultural intelligence becomes a key part of their career development.

Margaret's two-year immersion in Japan and other Asian cultures had enormous effects on her. It was not just a two-year concentrated program in improving cultural intelligence. Simultaneously with her cultural learning, she was playing out major interrelated issues of relationships, lifestyle, and career. Her development took place on many fronts simultaneously. Margaret is very clear that there is no way she could have developed in the same ways by spending the same two years in her familiar British cultural environment.

Career Development

One of the features of Margaret's career so far is that she has made nearly all of her own decisions. This is not as common as one might guess. Expatriate assignments are often strongly company-controlled and provide either guidance or direction to employees in their career decisions. But many, like Margaret, prefer to be responsible for their own destinies and to develop their international careers in their own ways.

Margaret's and other young people's experiences of self-initiated overseas travel tell us that *you don't need to be in an international company to acquire cultural intelligence!* Margaret has become culturally intelligent and internationally mobile in her own way, through her own self-designed apprenticeship. And although she has focused initially on Japan, the likelihood is that her natural curiosity and developing CQ will in due course lead her into new, contrasting cross-cultural experiences elsewhere. Perhaps she will even become one of the growing number of "global citizens"—high CQ travelers who feel at home wherever they are. Cultural intelligence combined with global opportunity gives our young people promise of a new, exciting, nomadic way of life our parents and grandparents could not have dreamed of.

There is much that people—particularly young people—can do to prepare themselves for the likelihood of international experience during their careers. In some ways, the smaller and more isolated a country is, the greater the energy and drive of its citizens to see something different, and the more young people travel.

For example, Australians and New Zealanders, isolated as they are in the out-of-the way continent of Oceania, have an institution known as "the Big O.E." ("O.E." stands for "overseas experience"). Every year many thousands of their young people undertaking the Big O.E. pour overseas, mainly to Europe, without any career desire beyond seeing the world. Typically they have work permits for the UK but no specific jobs to go to. They make their way in the foreign environment as best they can, pumping gas and waiting tables or moving to higher-level work, until, after several years of this stimulation, they either return home culturally enriched or are enticed by superior career opportunities or new relationships to remain overseas. Research on returned O.E.-ers suggests that their learning—cross-cultural, vocational, and interpersonal—has been dramatic and is probably far superior to what they could have obtained by continuing their career development at home.[7]

As we indicated in Chapter 4, there are many O.E.-like strategies for young people from any country to enrich their careers and improve their cultural intelligence: study abroad, backpacker tourism, teaching their language overseas, humanitarian service (for example, the Peace Corps) are just a few. These are all excellent self-initiated ways of familiarizing yourself with overseas locations and increasing your cultural intelligence. If you are a middle-aged reader and are thinking, "Gee, I wish I had thought like that when I was young," it's never too late. Talk to your children about it!

Repatriation

You might not think coming home after living and working overseas would be difficult. However, the shock of returning home after a long period of time away is often more difficult to deal with than the initial culture shock of going abroad. This happens for a number of reasons. First of all, home has changed. When you return, the gradual changes that occurred in your country of origin while you were away confront you all at once, often confounding your expectations based on past experience. In addition, you too have changed. You may not realize it, but living and working overseas is likely to have had a dramatic effect on your attitudes, beliefs, and behavior. When you visit favorite places or friends, your new self is often confronted with memories or reflections of your old self. Much of this change in you is for the better, but adjusting to the fact that you are different is nonetheless stressful.

Complicating matters even further if you are an expatriate assignee is the fact that even returning to your old firm is often not what you expected. Consider the following case.

RETURNING TO AN UNCERTAIN FUTURE

Karl-Heinz leans back on the bench and stares out across the expanse of Central Park. He reflects on his seven-year assignment to the New York office of Kuselbanc. Professionally, things have gone extremely well for him. When he arrived, the New York division was right at the beginning of a boom phase. His first promotion came unexpectedly after only eight months. In order to secure a second promotion he extended his assignment. But his real break came in his fifth year when his boss retired and Karl-Heinz was made head of the corporate finance department.

Unfortunately, things have not gone so well for Karl-Heinz's wife, Gretchen. Gretchen finds the New York way of life frenetic and selfish compared with the quiet, orderly existence she enjoyed in Dusseldorf. She has been unable to get a work permit and has become increasingly discontented with her life as a housewife and with Karl-Heinz's increased travel schedule. Also, his two daughters (now nine and five) have no real connection to Germany and consider themselves Americans. The death of Gretchen's father and her mother's wish to have her daughter near her have made staying in New York increasingly difficult for Gretchen.

After several weeks of consideration, Karl-Heinz and Gretchen have decided to return to Germany. But it has now taken over nine months for Kuselbanc to find a position for him. Karl-Heinz feels anger well up inside him as he considers whether to take the job at last being offered him back in Germany. The branch-manager position would be at little more than half his New York salary, and he would be posted to Eastern Germany, where he would be out of touch with all the important decisions made at headquarters. This is the reality of the "challenging" return assignment the corporate HR department had promised to find for him on his return. If they have a plan at all for repatriating expatriates, he thinks, it seems to be to punish those who are really committed to the organization. They assign you to one of those programs for high fliers and send you abroad, but there is no career planning whatsoever. Their slogan that internationally experienced managers are important to the organization and that international experience is a prerequisite to senior management is garbage. Karl-Heinz sighs bitterly.[8]

Unfortunately, Karl-Heinz's situation is not unique or even unusual. Generally, repatriates report that an overseas assignment, while personally rewarding and often beneficial to their cultural intelligence, has not had a positive effect on their careers in their firms. Reports are common that expatriates, as well as being culturally destabilized, are often neglected on return. They are put in "holding patterns," offered inferior assignments, and are not valued for their international experience and increased cross-cultural abilities. One study found that one in four returning expatriates left their employers shortly after reentry.[9] In these cases both the employees and the firms are losers. Employees lose promised advancement, and the firms lose the knowledge and skills—and of course the increased CQ—of the returning expatriates.

Offsetting these negatives is the dramatic personal growth reported by returnees. The following quotes from actual returnees are typical.

"I have learned more about myself than I can accurately put into words, but suffice to say it has been an all-around positive experience for my personal development."

"I have learned to look at the world around me with a childlike wonder and to drop any preconceived notions I may have been holding. I have learned that just because I have grown up indoctrinated by a certain set of rules regarding how relationships and society in general work, that does not make them universally true or right."

"Living and working there is not for the faint of heart, and you had better be sure you have an adventurous spirit before you commit, but it is an unforgettable experience."

Acquiring CQ Through Overseas Experiences

As suggested by these comments from returnees, spending a significant amount of time living and working overseas is an important way of developing cultural intelligence. But it will not happen automatically. You will have to focus on it. You will have to prepare. You will have to be mindful. Every cross-cultural incident, at your work, in social life, even when shopping, will be an opportunity to reflect, to learn, and to experiment.

You will need to be in the right frame of mind to acquire CQ. Why are you going overseas? What do you want from the experience? Escaping a bad situation at home or hoping for career advancement on return may not be the best motivation. Self-development, a desire for adventure, a wish to broaden your horizons and meet new people, or a sense of mission are better. They will help you to live in the here-and-now and to take a genuine interest in your new environment and the people you meet.

You will need to prepare. Read all you can about the new country you are to visit. Find out about its cultural background, using literature like that recommended at the end of this book. Study the cultural dimensions we introduced in Chapter 2, and try to figure out where your new home fits in. Seek out people who have been there, and ask them about their experiences.

Remember that the most common reasons that people return early from overseas revolve around family issues. If you have family members who are going overseas with you, involve them in the preparation, and support them in the adventure. It is their opportunity to acquire cultural intelligence too. Your partner's adjustment is just as important as your own. For your children, an international move is a unique opportunity to grow CQ. Being young, they will have fewer fixed beliefs, less cultural cruise control. It is an ideal opportunity for them to learn quickly. However, children sometimes need guidance to avoid becoming completely absorbed in the new culture. They may need help in learning to understand that the essence of cultural intelligence is to be able to respond to different cultural situations without losing one's own identity.

You will have to be self-forgiving and patient. Even with plenty of preparation you will doubtless make many initial mistakes. No matter how culturally intelligent you are, you will need time to adjust. Your performance in the first year overseas is unlikely to be your best. You will probably need to laugh at your own inadequacies from time to time and to remember that every experience, even the most negative, has its own potential for learning.

The future for many is not just intercultural but international. We, and our children, will more and more have to be able to feel at home wherever we are and to function with the ease and familiarity that is habitual to us on home soil. The opportunity to travel overseas is precious. The investment is our time and aspirations and the energy we give to the process. Part of the dividend we receive is enhanced cultural intelligence. As we hope this book has shown, the reward is well worth the effort.

Summary

This chapter considers the paradoxical relationship between cultural intelligence and international career moves such as expatriate assignments and self-initiated overseas travel. On the one hand, a period of time living and working overseas is one of the best ways to improve cultural intelligence. On the other, to be productive overseas one needs cultural intelligence. The key to managing this paradox is embodied in the cultural intelligence model of knowledge, mindfulness, and skilled behavior. It is important to know a good deal about yourself and your motivation before undertaking an overseas experience. It is also important to understand how the phenomenon of culture shock and the process of adjustment affect your attitudes and behavior. Practicing mindfulness enhances this ability. The behavioral and other skills acquired and tested in an extended period abroad can have a dramatic influence on your career. Expatriation and repatriation both carry potential benefits of career development but also risks of career disruption. The days of stable, easily identifiable career paths are past, particularly in global careers. Career travel may bring unpredicted but exciting new opportunities. To be offered such opportunities and to be able to take them, you will need to develop a set of marketable skills and attributes needed for success, such as cultural intelligence. So armed, you can seize the many opportunities that are presented by today's dynamic international business environment.

The Essentials of Cultural Intelligence

Business in the twenty-first century is global, and the need to deal effectively with others who are culturally different has become a business necessity. This globalization is being fueled by dramatic economic shifts in many countries and by advances in communications technology. We may not travel the globe to do business, but the world has come to us. Daily we have to deal with international issues and with people from other countries and cultures.

Despite the rapid modernization of the world, culture is slow to change. For the foreseeable future, cultural differences will remain a key factor in interpersonal interactions. And we have long known that interacting effectively with others is the most important part of a manager's job.

In an increasingly competitive world, managers who do not keep their skills up-to-date run the risk of losing out. In this book we have introduced what we believe to be the key managerial competency for the twenty first century, *cultural intelligence*. Cultural intelligence, the capability to deal effectively with people from different cultural backgrounds, is a multifaceted competency consisting of cultural *knowledge*, the practice of *mindfulness*, and a repertoire of *behavioral skills*. As shown in the figure that we introduced in Chapter 4, cultural intelligence is developed in an experiential, iterative way in which each repetition of the cycle builds on the previous one.

The feedback from each cycle of experience leads to an everhigher CQ. In this way specific knowledge gained in both formal and informal ways is transformed into skills that can then be applied to a variety of new situations.

Culture has a profound influence on almost all aspects of human endeavor. The culturally intelligent manager understands the possible effects of cultural variation in his or her own behavior and that of others. The culturally intelligent manager also knows how and in what circumstances these cultural differences are likely to exert their effect. Culture matters, but it doesn't matter to the same degree in all circumstances all the time.

Cultural intelligence also requires the practice of mindfulness. Mindfulness is being aware of our own assumptions, ideas, and emotions; noticing what is apparent about the other person's assumptions, words, and behavior; using all of the senses in perceiving situations; viewing the situation from several perspectives; attending to the context to help to interpret what is happening; creating new mental maps of others; creating new and more sophisticated categories for others; seeking out fresh information to confirm or disconfirm the mental maps; and using empathy.

Knowledge and mindfulness are key elements of cultural intelligence, but in themselves they are not enough. Becoming culturally intelligent means acquiring behavioral skills. It is not about becoming more skilled, but about developing a repertoire of skilled behaviors and knowing when to use each one.

While everyone can learn to be culturally intelligent, certain characteristics of individuals support the development of cultural intelligence. These are integrity, openness, and hardiness.

Culturally intelligent *decision makers* understand how people with different cultural backgrounds mentally simplify the complex decision-making process. They know their own motivation and goals in making decisions and understand how the motivation, goals, and decision-making methods of people from other cultures might be different from their own. They are mindful of the ethical components of business decisions and the relationship of ethical behavior to their underlying cultural values. Finally, they are able to adapt decision behavior such as the type and amount of information gathered, the weighting of decision criteria, and the degree of participation in decisions to the specific cultural context, while at the same time respecting the universal rights of human beings.

Culturally intelligent *negotiators* know that cultural differences have a huge influence on the communication process that underpins all negotiations. Managers spend much of their time in communication with others, and in no other activity is people's cultural grounding more influential. Both language and nonverbal behavior make it tricky to communicate across cultures. Culturally intelligent negotiators have the knowledge required to anticipate communication differences, practice mindfulness by paying attention to both the context and the conventions of communication as well as its content, and adapt their negotiation behavior to make concessions, persuade, exchange information, and/or build relationships, as appropriate for the negotiation and cultural context.

Culturally intelligent *leaders* know that leadership exists largely in the minds of followers. While all followers expect leaders to have a vision, to be able to communicate that vision, and to have skill in organizing followers, the specific behaviors that indicate these abilities vary dramatically across cultures. The culturally intelligent leader understands that his or her leadership style will be largely either task- or relationship-oriented but that some adaptation of this style may be required depending on the needs of followers (for example, their degree of collectivism). Culturally intelligent leaders do not unthinkingly mimic the leadership behaviors of another culture. Rather, they pay close attention to leaders like themselves who are effective in the cross-cultural environment and model their behavior appropriately.

Culturally intelligent *team management* means knowing that culturally diverse workgroups and teams have the potential for very high achievement but that they also have characteristics that make them prone to failure. The key to managing culturally diverse workgroups is maximizing the benefits of diversity while at the same time minimizing the costs. Culturally intelligent team management also requires fostering cultural intelligence among team members. In order to do this, team members and team leaders must understand how groups develop and the effects of group processes as well as the steps to cultural intelligence. Team managers must consider the effects of group type, the nature of the group task, the degree and nature of the cultural diversity in the group, and the extent to which the group has developed the necessary internal processes to resolve conflict.

Culturally intelligent *career management* means knowing that the nature of careers and the relationship between individuals and firms is changing. These changes require careful management of overseas experiences if these events are to have a positive effect on the development of cultural intelligence and your long-term career. You need to be able to manage the apparent paradox that overseas assignments are a key way of developing cultural intelligence, but that cultural intelligence is also a requirement for success on these endeavors. This involves knowing your motivation and underlying traits, deciding where overseas experience fits with your long-term career plans, and carefully considering factors such as family issues and how your success will be evaluated. For a person seeking cultural intelligence, a period of time living and working overseas, either self-initiated or as a company assignment, can be extremely rewarding.

We wish that we could somehow endow you with cultural

intelligence or that you could download it from the Internet. But developing cultural intelligence involves hard work on your part. It is essentially an experiential process. As such it is often both physically and emotionally taxing. However, we think the feelings of confidence and control in cross-cultural interactions that you will feel are worth the effort. We hope this book has helped to start you on this journey.

Where to Get
Country Information

The purpose of this book is to help readers begin a journey toward a new way of thinking and being with respect to different cultures. However, we recognize that our "process view" of effective cross-cultural interaction by becoming *culturally intelligent* is based on some knowledge of specific cultural differences. Moreover, doing business in other countries often requires a deep understanding of economic, legal, and political conditions, as well as culture. With this need in mind, we have provided the following list of websites and book series. The list of websites is a baker's dozen web addresses that we have found useful. Please note that they are biased toward U.S. and Canadian sites because these are the ones we use. There are comparable sites in other regions (particularly Europe) that offer similar information.

Also listed are book series that are devoted to helping one to do business in specific countries or regions. These books have their place in developing cultural intelligence. However, we caution readers that the vast majority of these books are written from a Western perspective and may overlook certain critical aspects of cultural difference. Their content and depth of coverage vary widely. You should use these books with caution and expect that your own experience could be very different from that described.

Internet Sites

1. *Country Background Notes* (U.S. State Dept.) *Background Notes* are factual publications that contain information on all the countries of the world with which the United States maintains relations. They include facts on the country's land, people, history, government, political conditions, economy, and its relations with other countries and the United States. The *Notes* are updated/revised by the Office of Electronic Information and Publications of the Bureau of Public Affairs as they are received from regional bureaus and are added to the database of the Department of State website.

   http://www.state.gov/r/pa/ei/bgn/

2. *Country Commercial Guides* (U.S. Dept. of Commerce) The Country Commercial Guides (CCG) are prepared by U.S. embassy staff once a year and contain information on the business and economic situations of foreign countries and the political climates as they affect U.S. business. Each CCG contains the same chapter organization and an appendix, which include topics such as marketing, trade regulations, investment climate, and business travel.

   http://www.usatrade.gov/website/ccg.nsf/
   ccghomepage?openform

3. *Country Studies: Area Handbook Series* This website contains the online versions of books previously published in hard copy by the Federal Research Division of the Library of Congress under the Country Studies/Area Handbook Program sponsored by the U.S. Army. Because the original intent of the series' sponsor was to focus primarily on lesser-known areas of the world or regions in which U.S. forces might be deployed, the series is not all-inclusive. At present, 102 countries and regions are covered. Notable omissions include Canada, France, the United Kingdom, and other Western nations, as well as a number of African nations. The date of information for each country appears on the title

page of the section for each country and at the end of each section of text. This site is a good source for information about non-Western countries but doesn't usually have current data. The material is useful as background information.

http://lcweb2.loc.gov/frd/cs/cshome.html

4. *Department of Foreign Affairs and International Trade (Canada): Market Reports* Through this site DFAIT provides free access to hundreds of sectoral market studies and country-specific reports prepared by its Market Research Centre and by its offices abroad. These reports are intended to help Canadian companies identify foreign business opportunities and learn more about their target markets. You must register for a (free) password to access many of the DFAIT market reports. Look for your country, choose one of the links to relevant Canadian consulates and embassies in the country, then click on the link to Industry Sector Market Reports & Links. Also at the consulate/embassy level, click on the Market Prospect link for data on business conditions and for advice on doing business in the country.

http://www.infoexport.gc.ca/ie-en/EServices.jsp

5. *Economist.com—Country Briefings* This site is a leading source of country briefing information. Covers sixty countries with succinct forecasts, economic and political profiles, core statistics, essential recent articles, and in-depth surveys from the *Economist*. Note that only some of the information is free.

http://www.economist.com/countries/

6. *Ernst & Young* EY publishes reports that cover the tax details (and related country information) associated with doing business in over 130 countries, but it tends to bury them pretty deeply at its site. Click on Select a Country/Region in the top left corner of the EY site, then click on Issues and Perspectives. Look for a link to a "library" or to further tax details on your country. Sometimes you will get lucky enough to get a full "Doing Business in" guide, such as the one for China. For many other countries you are

lucky to get a shorter "Business and Investment Guide," such as the one for Kazakhstan.

http://www.ey.com/global/content.nsf/International/Home

7. *Industry Canada* (3 links)

Trade and Investment Country reports, prepared by the International Cooperation Directorate, provide a quick overview of business conditions in selected countries Canada trades with and opportunities for Canadian firms.

http://strategis.ic.gc.ca/epic/internet/inibi-iai.nsf/vwGeneratedInterE/h_bi18601e.html

Trade Data Online This site offers the ability to generate customized reports on Canadian and U.S. trade with over 200 countries—by product and by industry.

http://strategis.gc.ca/sc_mrkti/tdst/engdoc/tr_homep.html

Market Research This site provides Canadian and U.S. resources on international markets. Check for publication dates as some of these reports are outdated. You can get the newest U.S. reports from the U.S. Department of Commerce site listed above.

http://strategis.ic.gc.ca/sc_mrkti/ibinddc/engdoc/1a1.html

8. *International Monetary Fund (IMF) Country Information* Staff Country Reports, press releases, and occasional/working papers on almost every country. If you are quoted a price when you click on something, look for a link to the PDF full-text version—it should be free. The Staff Country Reports are particularly good, but they can be lengthy. Save time by checking the table of contents of the PDF files for the pages with tables and charts.

http://www.imf.org/external/country/index.htm

9. *International Trade Administration (US)* The ITA page has resources to help U.S. businesses compete globally. These resources, including guides to doing business in many countries as well as trade and economic statistics, may help you as well. This site includes access to the U.S. government's

Country Commercial Guides as well as to Market Access and Compliance information for many countries.

http://www.ita.doc.gov/

10. *PriceWaterhouseCoopers: Doing Business and Investing in . . .* Each month PWC focuses on a different country—providing an up-to-the-minute look at what it means to do business there. The site includes a look at a country's business environment, foreign investment and trade opportunities, its regulatory environment, labor practices, financial system, tax laws, and more.

http://www.pwcglobal.com/Extweb/NewCoAtWork.nsf/docid/5DCFF8E317E993D585256A770051ACB8

11. *Surf the World (formerly E-Thologies)* The Canadian Department of Foreign Affairs & International Trade's Centre for Intercultural Learning has created a website with information on more than 200 countries. It covers social, political, economic, environmental, and cultural issues. The *cultural insights* section of this site is particularly noteworthy. It provides commentary from both a local national and a Canadian about the culture of each country. The background of each *cultural interpreter* is provided in some detail so that you can gain a deeper understanding of the individual's perspective.

http://www.e-thologies.com/menu-en.asp

12. *United Nations Industrial Development Organization: Country Information* The UNIDO offers basic data on most countries of the world (GDP, manufactured exports, manufacturing value added, and so on) as well as more detailed statistics such as labor productivity and wage rates by industry. (Choose a country, and then click on Statistics for the more detailed data.)

http://www.unido.org/Regions.cfm?area=GLO

13. *World Bank Group: Country Data* Tables drawn from the World Bank Development Indicators give quick reference numbers for 206 countries as well as various regional

groupings. This site also includes some links to other useful international agency sites that have additional information.

http://www.worldbank.org/data/countrydata/countrydata.html

Book Series

Graphic Arts Center Publishing, *Culture Shock Guides*. Often written by expatriates or travelers.

Greenwood Publishing Group, *Culture and Customs Series*. In-depth coverage of a variety of countries, each by different experts, covering history, religion, customs, media, and the arts from a predominantly anthropological perspective.

Interlink Publishing, *In Focus Travel Guides*. As the name implies, but with broader coverage of people, culture, politics, government, economics, religion, and so on.

McGraw-Hill, *Comparative Societies Series*. A series of short books providing material on comparative societies, comparative politics, comparative economics. The opening chapter of each establishes historical and cultural context, while subsequent chapters focus on the basic institutions, social stratification, social problems, and social change.

Survival Books, *Living and Working in . . .* Series (15 countries) Practical advice for expatriates, retirees, prospective home buyers, and so on.

World Trade Press, *Country Business Guides Series* (12 countries), *Passport to the World Series* (25 countries), and the *Global Road Warrior* (97 countries) all contain useful information.

Notes

CHAPTER I

1. Vignettes adapted from Cushner, K, & Brislin, R. W. (1996). *Intercultural interactions: A practical guide*. Thousand Oaks CA: Sage.

2. McLuhan, M. (1964). *Understanding media: The extensions of man*. New York: McGraw-Hill.

3. Our definition of globalization is drawn from our colleague Barbara Parker's work on this topic in *Globalization: Managing across boundaries*. London: Sage.

4. For examples see the following: Hofstede, G. (1980). *Culture's consequences: International differences in work related values*. Beverly Hills, CA: Sage; Schwartz, S. H. (1992). Universals in the content and structure of values: Theoretical advances and empirical tests in 20 countries. In M. P. Zanna (Ed.), *Advances in Experimental Social Psychology* (pp. 1–65). San Diego: Academic Press; Trompenaars, F. (1993). *Riding the waves of culture*. Burr Ridge, IL: Irwin; and Triandis, H. C. (1972). *The analysis of subjective culture*. New York: Wiley.

5. While this concept has gone by various names over the years, including intercultural competence, global mindset, and global competencies, the definition of the idea as a special type of intelligence can be attributed to Chris Earley in his 2002 article, Redefining interactions across cultures and organizations:

Moving forward with cultural intelligence. *Research in Organizational Behavior,* 24, pp. 271–299 and in his 2003 book with Soon Ang, *Cultural intelligence: Individual interactions across cultures.* Stanford, CA: Stanford University Press.

6. There is, at present, no accepted measure of cultural intelligence. However, the authors of this book are engaged in a major research project to create and test such a measure.

CHAPTER 2

1. Adapted from Cushner, K., & Brislin, R. W. (1996). *Intercultural interactions: A practical guide.* Thousand Oaks, CA: Sage.

2. Hofstede, G. (1980). *Culture's consequences: International differences in work related values.* Beverly Hills, CA: Sage.

3. PTA is the common abbreviation for Parent Teacher Association.

4. For an interesting discussion of organizational culture see Deal, T., & Kennedy, A. (1982). *Corporate culture: The rites and rituals of corporate life.* Reading, MA: Addison-Wesley.

5. For more information on the process of acculturation see Berry, J. W. (1990). The psychology of acculturation: Understanding individuals moving between cultures. In R. Brislin (Ed.), *Cross-cultural research and methodology series: Vol. 14. Applied cross-cultural psychology* (pp. 232–252). Newbury Park, CA: Sage.

6. The metaphor of an iceberg to represent culture comes from Schein, E. H. (1985). *Organizational culture and leadership.* San Francisco: Jossey-Bass.

7. The idea of tight and loose cultures comes from Pelto, P. J. (1968). The difference between tight and loose societies. *Transaction,* April, 37–40 cited in Triandis, H. C. (1995). *Individualism and collectivism.* Boulder, CO: Westview.

8. For a more complete discussion of convergence versus divergence of culture, see Smith, P. B., & Bond, M. H. (1999). *Social psychology across cultures.* Boston: Allyn and Bacon; and Ralston, D. A., Holt, D. H., Terpstra, R. H., & Yu, K. (1997). The impact of national culture and economic ideology on managerial work values: A study of the United States, Russia, Japan, and China. *Journal of International Business Studies,* 28(1), 177–207.

9. Adapted from Cushner, K., & Brislin, R. W. (1996). *Intercultural interactions: A practical guide* (2nd. Edition). Thousand Oaks, CA: Sage.

10. The method used by Geert Hofstede in his groundbreaking study is not without its critics. See for example, Roberts, K. H., & Boyacigiller, N. A. (1984). Cross national organizational research: The grasp of the blind men. In B. M. Staw & L. L. Cummings (Eds.), *Research in Organizational Behavior* (Vol. 6, pp. 423–475). Greenwich, CT: JAI Press; and Dorfman, P. W., & Howell, J. P. (1988). Dimensions of national culture and effective leadership patterns: Hofstede revisited. *Advances in International Comparative Management, 3,* 127–150.

11. For additional information about these dimensions of culture, how they were derived, and the process of creating the map shown in Figure 2.2, see Sagiv, L., & Schwartz, S. H. (1995). Value priorities and readiness for out-group social contact. *Journal of Personality and Social Psychology, 69,* 437–448; Schwartz, S. H. (1992). Universals in the content and structure of values: Theoretical advances and empirical tests in 20 countries. In M. P. Zanna (Ed.), *Advances in experimental social psychology* (pp. 1–65). San Diego: Academic Press; Schwartz, S. H. (1994). Beyond individualism/collectivism: New dimensions of values. In U. Kim, H. C. Triandis, C. Kagitçibasi, S. C. Choi, and G. Yoon (Eds.), *Individualism and collectivism: Theory, applications, and methods* (pp. 85–119). Newbury Park, Ca: Sage; and Schwartz, S. H., & Bilsky, W. (1990). Toward a universal psychological structure of human values. *Journal of Personality and Social Psychology, 53,* 550–562.

12. The dimensions of individualism and collectivism have been used to explain and predict a diverse array of social behavior. However, some scholars have suggested that they have been overused and that other dimensions have been neglected. For example, see Earley, P. C., & Gibson. C. B. (1998). Taking stock in our progress on individualism-collectivism: 100 years of solidarity and community. *Journal of Management, 24,* 265–304.

13. An extensive review of the causes and consequences of individualism and collectivism, including the relationship to affluence, family structure, health, religion, and politics, is contained in Triandis (1995). *Individualism and collectivism.* Boulder, CO: Westview.

1. For more information on psychological scripts see Abelson, R. P. (1981). Psychological status of the script concept. *American Psychologist, 36*, 715–729; Gioa, D. A., & Poole, P. P. (1984). Scripts in organizational behaviour. *Academy of Management Review, 9*, 449–459; and Lord, R. G., & Kernan, M. C. (1987). Scripts as determinants of purposeful behavior in organizations. *Academy of Management Review, 12*, 265–277.

2. Mindfulness is a concept that originated in Zen Buddhism. To learn more about the concept from this perspective, see the writings of the Buddhist monk Thich Nhat Hanh, especially *The miracle of mindfulness* (1999). Boston: Beacon Press and *Peace is every step: The path of mindfulness in everyday life* (1991). New York: Bantam Books. Mindfulness was introduced into psychology literature by Ellen Langer in her excellent book *Mindfulness* (1989). Cambridge, MA: Perseus Books.

3. The role models that are appropriate vary from culture to culture and are affected by such things as social class and gender. For example, it is much more appropriate for a young U.S. woman to model herself after a business executive than it would be for a Japanese woman, and a tennis player would be a more desirable role model for an upper-class English boy than would a football (soccer) player.

4. The section on how culture affects behavior draws heavily on Thomas, D. C. (2002). *Essentials of international management: A cross-cultural perspective.* Thousand Oaks, CA: Sage.

5. Our approach to treating stereotypes as a natural outcome of social categorization is consistent with classic work on this topic. For example, see Ashmore, R. D., & Del Boca, F. K. (1981). Conceptual approaches to stereotypes and stereotyping. In D. L. Hamilton (Ed.), *Cognitive processes in stereotyping and intergroup behavior* (pp. 1–35). Hillsdale, NJ: Erlbaum.

6. Without wishing in any way to ignore or diminish the dreadful effects of racism in many countries round the world, in this book we assume that our readers do not harbor racist attitudes. That is, they acknowledge differences between groups but do not assume these differences imply superiority or inferiority. They may experience lack of understanding of other cultures and sometimes puzzlement, apprehension, even fear. But they do

not feel antagonism, and to the extent that they do, they seek to overcome it. In this book we are assuming that readers have moved beyond the negative attitudes of racism and genuinely seek to manifest their recognition of the equality of all groups and their goodwill toward others, in better understanding of these groups and improving relationships with them.

7. Adapted from Cushner K., & Brislin, R. W. (1996). *Intercultural interactions: A practical guide*. Thousand Oaks, CA: Sage.

8. We recognize that firms may have rules that define certain activities as bribes, which of course influence the perceptions of their employees. However, these rules themselves may be a sort of corporate mindlessness.

9. The idea of a repertoire of behaviors as a way to define the behavioral component of cultural intelligence resulted from numerous discussions with members of the International Organizations Network (ION), particularly Allan Bird, Mark Mendenhall, Joyce Osland, Nakiye Boyacigiller, and Schon Beechlor.

CHAPTER 4

1. The term "matrix in the minds of managers" was first used to describe the idea of a global mindset in a quote from an anonymous manager in Bartlett, C. A., & Ghoshal, S. (1989). *Managing across borders: The transnational solution* (p. 195). Boston: Harvard Business School Press.

2. Adapted from a case in Napier, N. K., & Thomas, D. C. (2004). *Managing relationships in transition economies*. New York: Praeger.

3. These three characteristics are drawn from a chapter on global competencies by Joyce Osland and Allan Bird in Mendenhall, M., Lane, H., Maznevski, M., & McNett, J. (Eds.), (2003). *Handbook of cross-cultural management*. Oxford: Blackwell.

4. For additional information on the inadequacy of stereotypes and the need to understand them in context, see an excellent article by Joyce Osland and Allan Bird, Beyond sophisticated stereotyping: Cultural sense making in context. In D. C. Thomas (Ed.) (2003), *Readings and cases in international management: A cross-cultural perspective* (pp. 58–70). Thousand Oaks, CA: Sage.

5. This diagram is adapted from an idea first presented in Vijay Govindarajan and Anil Gupta's excellent book on global strategy, *The quest for global dominance* (2001). San Francisco: Jossey-Bass.

6. The concept of social learning was introduced by Albert Bandura. For a more extensive discussion, see Bandura, A. (1977). *Social learning theory*. Englewood Cliffs, NJ: Prentice-Hall.

7. Adapted from a case by Govindarajan & Gupta (2001: 126).

8. Vance, C. M. (2002). Analysis of self-initiating career path strategies: Similarities and differences across genders. Paper presented to the annual meeting of the Academy of Management, Seattle, WA.

9. Adapted from a case in Napier & Thomas (2004).

CHAPTER 5

1. For additional information on rational decision making in management and its limitations, see Bazerman, M. (1998). *Judgement in managerial decision making,* 4th Edition. New York: John Wiley & Sons.

2. The problems associated with rational models presented here are based on the concept of bounded rationality. See March, J. G. (1978). Bounded rationality, ambiguity, and the engineering of choice. *Bell Journal of* Economics, 9 (2), 587–608; and March, J., & Simon, H. (1958). *Organizations*. New York: Wiley.

3. The notion of heuristics presented here is derived from a classic article by Amos Tversky and Daniel Kahneman. Judgement under uncertainty: Heuristics, and biases. *Science, 85,* 1124–1131; and from Nisbett, R. E. & Ross, L. (1980). *Human inference*. Englewood Cliffs, NJ: Prentice-Hall.

4. These motivational biases are based on the effects of differences in the self-concepts of culturally different individuals. See, for example, Erez, M., & Earley, P. C. (1993). *Culture, self-identity, and work*. New York: Oxford University Press.

5. Bontempo, R., Lobel, S. A., & Triandis, H. C. (1990). Compliance and value internalization in Brazil and the U.S.: Effects of allocentrism and anonymity. *Journal of Cross-Cultural Psychology*, 21, 200–213.

6. See, for example, Heine, S. J., & Lehman, D. R. (1995). Cultural variation in unrealistic optimism: Does the West feel more invulnerable than the East? *Journal of Personality and Social Psychology,* 68, 595–607; and Miyamoto, Y. & Ktayama, S. (2002). Cultural variation in correspondence bias: The critical role of attitude diagnosticity and socially constrained behavior. *Journal of Personality and Social Psychology,* 83 (5), 1239–1248.

7. Adapted from a case by Shekshnia, S. V., & Puffer, S. M. (2003). Rus Wane equipment: Joint venture in Russia. In D. C. Thomas (Ed.), *Readings and cases in international management: A cross-cultural perspective.* Thousand Oaks: CA: Sage.

8. *Guanxi* is often translated as a network of relationships. It is, however, an indigenous Chinese construct that can only be properly understood within the Chinese context. See for example Gold T., Guthrie, D., & Wank, D. (Eds.) (2002). *Social connections in China: Institutions, culture, and the changing nature of Guanxi.* Cambridge: Cambridge University Press.

9. Shackleton, V., & Newell, S. (1994). European management selection methods: A comparison of five countries. *International Journal of Selection and Assessment,* 2, 91–102.

10. For more information on this central ethical question, see Donaldson, T. (1989). *The ethics of international business.* New York: Oxford University Press.

11. The idea of a set of fundamental human rights that are invariant across cultures is central to moving beyond cultural relativism. See Donaldson (1989), but also, Donaldson, T. (1996). Values in tension: Ethics away from home. *Harvard Business Review*, Sept./Oct., 48–62.

CHAPTER 6

1. Condensed from cases by Cushner, K. & Brislin, R. W. (1996). *Intercultural interactions: A practical guide.* Thousand Oaks, CA: Sage Publications.

2. The idea of cultural grounding in communication comes from Clark, H. H., & Brennan, S. E. (1991). Grounding in communication. *Perspectives on socially shared communication.* Washington, D.C.: American Psychological Association.

3. Estimates of the number of languages in the world vary between two and ten thousand. However, the number in use by

significant numbers of people is many fewer. In many countries there are at least two native languages and in some cases, such as Papua New Guinea, there are hundreds.

4. The question of the optimal age to learn a foreign language has long been studied. For more information, see Asher, J. J., & Garcia, R. (1969). The optimal age to learn a foreign language. *Modern Language Journal, 53,* 334–341. There is little debate, however, about the fact that children pick up new languages "naturally" while older learners generally have to struggle long and hard to achieve even moderate fluency.

5. Adapted from a situation described in Napier, N. K., & Thomas, D. C. (2004). *Managing relationships in transition economies.* New York: Praeger.

6. See, for example, Giles, H., Taylor, D. M., & Bourhis, R. Y. (1973). Towards a theory of interpersonal accommodation through speech: Some Canadian data. *Language in Society, 2,* 177–192.

7. See Felson, R. B. (1978). Aggression is impression management. *Social Psychology Quarterly, 41,* 259–281, cited in Smith, P. B., & Bond, M. H. (1999). *Social psychology across cultures.* Boston: Allyn and Bacon.

8. This example taken from an interesting, informative, and humorous look at the English language by Bill Bryson (2001). *The mother tongue: English and how it got that way.* New York: Harper Collins.

9. This list of second-language strategies is adapted from Adler, N. J., & Kiggundu, M. N. (1983). Awareness at the crossroad: Designing translator based training programs. In D. Landis & R. Brislin (Eds.), *Handbook of intercultural training.* Elmsford, NY: Pergamon Press.

10. Adapted from Irving, D., & Inkson, K. (1998) *It must be Watties.* Auckland: David Bateman.

11. Engholm, C. (1991). *When business East meets business West: The guide to practice and protocol in the Pacific Rim.* New York: John Wiley.

12. This anecdote was adapted from a case study by Joseph DiStefano (2003). Johannes van den Bosch sends an e-mail, in D. C. Thomas (Ed.), *Readings and cases in international management: A cross-cultural perspective.* Thousand Oaks, CA: Sage.

13. The idea of social distance or, as it is also called, prox-

emics, is drawn from Hall, E. T. (1966). *The hidden dimension*. Garden City, NY: Doubleday.

14. See, for example, Andersen, P. A., & Bowman, L. (1985). Positions of power: Nonverbal cues of status and dominance in organizational communication. Paper presented at the annual convention of the International Communication Association, Honolulu, HI; and Aronoff, J., Woike, B. A., & Hyman, L. M. (1992).Which are the stimuli in facial displays of anger and happiness? *Journal of Personality and Social Psychology. 62*, 1050– 1066.

15. Ekman, P. W. (1982). *Emotion in the human face,* 2nd Edition. Cambridge: Cambridge University Press.

16. Graham, J. L. (1987). A theory of interorganizational negotiations. *Research in Marketing, 9*, 163–183.

CHAPTER 7

1. While this is a Western definition of leadership (see Yukl, G. [1994]. *Leadership in organizations* 3rd Edition. Upper Saddle River, NJ: Prentice Hall), some international consensus seems to be building toward this definition. See House, R. J., Wright, N. S., & Aditya, R. N. (1997). Cross-cultural research on organizational leadership: A critical analysis and a proposed theory. In P. C. Earley & M. Erez (Eds.), *New perspectives on international industrial/organizational psychology* (pp. 535– 625). San Francisco: New Lexington Press.

2. As appealing as the idea may be, researchers have yet to find certain characteristics of individuals that are consistently related to leader emergence or leader effectiveness. For more on this topic, see Dorfman, P. W. (1996). International and crosscultural leadership. In J. Punnitt & O. Shenkar (Eds.), *Handbook for international management research* (pp. 276–349). Cambridge, MA: Blackwell.

3. See Dorfman (1996).

4. Al-Kubaisy, A. (1985). A model in the administrative development of Arab Gulf countries. *The Arab Gulf, 17*(2), 29–48.

5. Nakane, C. (1970). *Japanese society*. Berkeley: University of California Press.

6. Drucker, P. (1994). The new superpower: The overseas Chinese. *The Wall Street Journal,* (December 20), 17.

7. Sorge, A. (1993). Management in France. In D. Hickson (Ed.), *Management in Western Europe: Society, culture and organization in twelve nations* (pp. 65–87). New York: Walter de Gruyter.

8. See Puffer, S. M. (1994). A portrait of Russian business leaders. *Academy of Management Executive,* 8(1), 41–54; and Napier, N. K., & Thomas, D. C. (2004). *Managing relationships in transition economies.* New York: Praeger.

9. Management by objectives (MBO) is a management technique based on the findings of goal-setting theory. For more information on this topic, see Locke, E. A., & Latham, G. P. (1984). *Goal setting: A motivational technique that works.* Englewood, Cliffs, NJ: Prentice-Hall; and Erez, M., & Earley, P. C. (1987). Comparative analysis of goal setting strategies across cultures. *Journal of Applied Psychology,* 71, 658–665.

10. Adapted from an unpublished case by Stanislav V. Shekshnia.

11. Adapted from a case by Barry Gold in Francesco, A. M., & Gold, B. A. (1998). *International organizational behavior: Text, readings, cases, and skills.* Upper Saddle River, NJ: Prentice-Hall.

12. For more information on transformational leadership, see Bass, B. M. (1985). *Leadership and performance beyond expectations.* New York: Free Press; and Conger, J. A., & Kanungo, R. (1988). *Charismatic leadership: The elusive factor in organizational effectiveness.* San Francisco: Jossey-Bass Publishers.

13. For example see House, R. J., Wright, N. S., & Aditya, R. N. (1997). Cross-cultural research on organizational leadership: A critical analysis and a proposed theory. In P. C. Earley & M. Erez (Eds.), *New perspectives on international industrial/organizational psychology* (pp. 535–625). San Francisco: New Lexington Press.

14. For an example of this effect, see Thomas, D. C., & Ravlin, E. C. (1995). Responses of employees to cultural adaptation by a foreign manager. *Journal of Applied Psychology,* 80, 133–146.

CHAPTER 8

1. In the Western world, the *hijab* has come to symbolize enforced silence. However, this is not a universal view among

Muslim women. Some see it as a woman's assertion that judgment of her physical person is to play no role in social interaction because by wearing it her appearance is not subjected to public scrutiny.

2. For more information on group processes, see Goodman, P. S., Paulin, E. C., & Schminke, M. (1987). Understanding groups in organizations. In B. Staw & L. Cummings (Eds.), *Research in organizational behavior* (Vol. 9, pp. 124–128). Greenwich, CT: JAI Press; and Hackman, J. R. (1991). *Groups that work (and those that don't)*. San Francisco: Jossey Bass.

3. See Arrow, H., & McGrath, J. E. (1995). Membership dynamics in groups at work: A theoretical framework. *Research in Organizational Behavior, 17*, 373–411.

4. For more information on this emerging topic, see an excellent book edited by Cris Gibson & Susan Cohen (2003). *Virtual teams that work: Creating conditions for virtual team effectiveness.* San Francisco: Jossey-Bass.

5. Janis, I. (1982). *Groupthink.* Boston: Houghton Mifflin.

6. Mullen, B., & Baumeister, R. F. (1987). Groups effects on self-attention and performance: Social loafing, social facilitation, and social impairment. In C. Hendrick (Ed.), *Review of personality and social psychology* (pp. 189–206). Newbury Park, CA: Sage.

7. This classic experiment is described in Ringelman, M. (1913). Recherches sur les moteurs animes: travails de l'homme. *Annales de l'Institut Nationale Agronomique, 12*, 1–40.

8. Process losses among individualists and collectivists also involve the extent to which the group members believe they are interacting with their in-group. For more on this topic, see Earley, P. C. (1989). Social loafing and collectivism: A comparison of the U.S. and the People's Republic of China. *Administrative Science Quarterly, 34*, 565–581; and Earley, P. C. (1993). East meets West meets Mid-East: Further explorations of collectivistic and individualistic work groups. *Academy of Management Journal, 36*, 319–348.

9. The three avenues of cultural influence on groups is described in more detail in Thomas, D. C., Ravlin, E. C., & Wallace, A.W. (1996). Effect of cultural diversity in work groups. *Research in Sociology of Organizations, 14*, 1–33.

10. For a summary of this research, see Goodman, P. S.,

Ravlin, E. C., & Argote, L. (1986). Current thinking about groups: Setting the stage for new ideas. In P. S. Goodman (Ed.), *Designing effective work groups*. San Francisco: Jossey-Bass.

11. Walker, R. (1999) Picnic in Samoa. In N. Monin, J. Monin, & R. Walker (Eds.) *Narratives of business and society: Differing New Zealand voices* (pp. 143–153). Auckland: Longman.

12. Nemeth, C. J. (1992). Minority dissent as a stimulant to group performance. In S. Worchel, W. Wood, & J. A. Simpson (Eds.), *Group process and productivity* (pp. 95–111). Newbury Park, CA: Sage.

13. For a more complete description of the effects of cultural distance see Thomas, D. C. (2002). *Essentials of international management: A cross-cultural perspective*. Thousand Oaks, CA: Sage.

14. Pearce, J. A., & Ravlin, E. C. (1987). The design and activation of self regulating work groups. *Human Relations, 11,* 751–782.

15. Tuckman, B. W. (1965). Developmental sequence in small groups. *Psychological Bulletin, 63* (6), 384–399.

16. The idea of "mapping" and then "bridging" across cultures is outlined in H. W. Lane, J. J. DiStefano, & M. L. Maznevski. (2000). *International management behavior*. Malden, MA: Blackwell.

CHAPTER 9

1. Adapted from Catlin, L. B. & White, T. F. (2001*). International business: Cultural sourcebook and case studies*. Cincinnati, OH: South-Western College Publishing.

2. For more information on the expatriate experience, see Thomas, D. C. (1998). The expatriate experience: A critical review and synthesis. *Advances in International Comparative Management, 12,* 237–273.

3. The idea that all expatriates go through a U-curve of adjustment was first presented in Lysgaard, S. (1955). Adjustment in a foreign society: Norwegian Fulbright grantees visiting the United States. *International Social Science Bulletin, 7,* 45–51; and Gullahorn, J. T., & Gullahorn, J. E. (1963) An extension of the U-curve hypothesis. *Journal of Social Issues, 19,* 33–47. However, recent research has suggested that this pattern of ad-

justment may be far from universal. See Black, J. S., & Mendenhall, M. (1991). The U-curve adjustment hypothesis revisited: A review and theoretical framework. *Journal of International Business Studies*, 22 (2), 225–247.

4. The phrase "very difficult" is classic Japanese understatement. New Zealanders would say "a bit of a worry" to express the same sentiment.

5. For example, one study found that some aspects of personality relate to the desire of expatriates to terminate their assignment and on supervisor rated performance; see Caligiuri, P. M. (2000). The big five personality characteristics as predictors of expatriates' desire to terminate the assignment and supervisor-rated performance. *Personnel Psychology*, 53, 67–88.

6. Thomas, D. C., Au, K., & Ravlin, E. C. (2003). Cultural variation and the psychological contract. *Journal of Organizational Behavior*, 24, 451–471.

7. See Inkson, K., Arthur, M. B., Pringle, J., & Barry, S. (1997). Expatriate assignment versus overseas experience: Contrasting models of international human resource development. *Journal of World Business*, 32 (4): 351–368.

8. Adapted from Stahl, G. H., & Mendenhall, M. E. (2003). Andreas Weber's reward for success in an expatriate assignment—A return to an uncertain future. In D. C. Thomas (Ed.), *Readings and cases in international management: A cross-cultural perspective* (pp. 371–734). Thousand Oaks, CA: Sage.

9. Adler, N. J. (1987). Pacific basin managers: A gaijin, not a woman. *Human Resource Management*, 26, 169–191.

Bibliography

Abelson, R. P. (1981). Psychological status of the script concept. *American Psychologist, 36,* 715–729.

Adler, N. J. (1987). Pacific basin managers: A gaijin, not a woman. *Human Resource Management, 26,* 169–191.

Adler, N. J., & Kiggundu, M. N. (1983). Awareness at the crossroad: Designing translator based training programs. In D. Landis, & R. Brislin (Eds.), *Handbook of intercultural training.* Elmsford, NY: Pergamon Press.

Al-Kubaisy, A. (1985). A model in the administrative development of Arab Gulf countries. *The Arab Gulf, 17* (2), 29–48.

Andersen, P. A., & Bowman, L. (1985). Positions of power: Nonverbal cues of status and dominance in organizational communication. Paper presented at the annual convention of the International Communication Association, Honolulu, HI.

Aronoff, J., Woike, B. A., & Hyman, L. M. (1992).Which are the stimuli in facial displays of anger and happiness? *Journal of Personality and Social Psychology, 62,* 1050–1066.

Arrow, H., & McGrath, J. E. (1993). Membership matters: How member change and continuity affect small group structure, process, and performance. *Small Group Research, 24,* 334–361.

Arrow, H., & McGrath, J. E. (1995). Membership dynamics in groups at work: A theoretical framework. *Research in Organizational Behavior, 17,* 373–411.

Asher, J. J., & Garcia, R. (1969). The optimal age to learn a foreign language. *Modern Language Journal, 53,* 334–341.

Ashmore, R. D., & Del Boca, F. K. (1981). Conceptual approaches to stereotypes and stereotyping. In D. L. Hamilton (Ed.), *Cognitive processes in stereotyping and intergroup behavior* (pp. 1–35). Hillsdale, NJ: Erlbaum.

Bandura, A. (1977). *Social learning theory.* Englewood Cliffs, NJ: Prentice-Hall.

Bartlett, C. A., & Ghoshal, S. (1989). *Managing across borders: The transnational solution.* Boston: Harvard Business School Press.

Bass, B. M. (1985). *Leadership and performance beyond expectation.* New York: Free Press.

Bazerman, M. (1998). *Judgement in managerial decision making,* 4th Edition. New York: John Wiley & Sons.

Berry, J. W. (1990). The psychology of acculturation: Understanding individuals moving between cultures. In R. Brislin (Ed.), *Cross-cultural research and methodology series: Vol. 14. Applied cross-cultural psychology* (pp. 232–252). Newbury Park, CA: Sage.

Black, J. S., & Mendenhall, M. (1991). The U-curve adjustment hypothesis revisited: A review and theoretical framework. *Journal of International Business Studies, 22,* 225–247.

Bontempo, R., Lobel, S. A., & Triandis, H. C. (1990). Compliance and value internalization in Brazil and the U.S.: Effects of allocentrism and anonymity. *Journal of Cross-Cultural Psychology, 21,* 200–213.

Bryson, B. (2001). *The mother tongue: English and how it got that way.* New York: HarperCollins.

Caligiuri, P. M. (2000). The big five personality characteristics as predictors of expatriates' desire to terminate the assignment and supervisor-rated performance. *Personnel Psychology, 53,* 67–88.

Catlin, L. B., & White, T. F. (2001). *International business: Cultural sourcebook and case studies.* Cincinnati, OH: South-Western College Publishing.

Clark, H. H., & Brennan, S. E. (1991). Grounding in communication. *Perspectives on Socially Shared Communication.* Washington, DC: American Psychological Association.

Conger, J. A., & Kanungo, R. (1988). *Charismatic leadership: The elusive factor in organizational effectiveness.* San Francisco: Jossey-Bass.

Cushner, K., & Brislin, R. W. (1996). *Intercultural interactions: A practical guide.* Thousand Oaks, CA: Sage

Deal, T., & Kennedy, A. (1982). *Corporate culture: The rites and rituals of corporate life.* Reading, MA: Addison-Wesley.

Donaldson, T. (1989). *The ethics of international business.* New York: Oxford University Press.

———. (1996). Values in tension: Ethics away from home. *Harvard Business Review,* Sept./Oct., 48–62.

Dorfman, P. W. (1996). International and cross-cultural leadership. In B. J. Punnitt & O. Shenkar (Eds.), *Handbook for international management research* (pp. 276–349). Cambridge, MA: Blackwell.

Dorfman, P. W., & Howell, J. P. (1988). Dimensions of national culture and effective leadership patterns: Hofstede revisited. *Advances in international comparative management, 3,* 127–150.

Drucker, P. (1994). The new superpower: The overseas Chinese. *Wall Street Journal,* (December 20), 17.

Earley, P. C. (1989). Social loafing and collectivism: A comparison of the U.S. and the People's Republic of China. *Administrative Science Quarterly, 34,* 565–581.

———. (1993). East meets West meets Mid-East: Further explorations of collectivistic and individualistic work groups. *Academy of Management Journal, 36,* 319–348.

———. (2002). Redefining interactions across cultures and organizations: Moving forward with cultural intelligence. *Research in Organizational Behavior, 24,* 271–299.

Earley, P. C., & Gibson. C. B. (1998). Taking stock in our progress on individualism-collectivism: 100 years of solidarity and community. *Journal of Management, 24,* 265–304.

Earley, P. C., & Ang, S. (2003). *Cultural intelligence: Individual interactions across cultures.* Stanford, CA: Stanford University Press.

Ekman, P. W. (1982). *Emotion in the human face,* 2nd Edition. Cambridge: Cambridge University Press.

Engholm, C. (1991). *When business East meets business West: The guide to practice and protocol in the Pacific rim.* New York: John Wiley & Sons.

Erez, M., & Earley, P. C. (1993). *Culture, self-identity, and work.* New York: Oxford University Press.

Felson, R. B. (1978). Aggression is impression management. *Social Psychology Quarterly, 41,* 259–281.

Francesco, A. M., & Gold, B. A. (1998). *International organizational behavior: Text, readings, cases, and skills.* Upper Saddle River, NJ: Prentice-Hall.

Gibson, C. B., & Cohen, S. G. (Eds.) (2003). *Virtual teams that work: Creating conditions for virtual team effectiveness.* San Francisco: Jossey-Bass.

Giles, H., Taylor, D. M., & Bourhis, R. Y. (1973). Towards a theory of interpersonal accommodation through speech: Some Canadian data. *Language in Society, 2,* 177–192.

Gioa, D. A., & Poole, P. P. (1984). Scripts in organizational behaviour. *Academy of Management Review, 9,* 449–459

Gold, T., Guthrie, D., & Wank, D. (Eds.) (2002). *Social connections in China : Institutions, culture, and the changing nature of Guanxi.* Cambridge: Cambridge University Press.

Goodman, P. S., Paulin, E. C., & Schminke, M. (1987). Understanding groups in organizations. In B. Staw & L. Cummings (Eds.), *Research in organizational behaviour* (Vol. 9, pp. 124–128). Greenwich, CT: JAI Press.

Goodman, P. S., Ravlin, E. C., & Argote, L. (1986). Current thinking about groups: Setting the stage for new ideas. In P. S. Goodman (Ed.), *Designing effective work groups.* San Francisco: Jossey-Bass.

Govindarajan, V., & Gupta, A. K. (2001). *The quest for global dominance.* San Francisco: Jossey-Bass.

Graham, J. L. (1987). A theory of interorganizational negotiations. *Research in Marketing, 9,* 163–183.

Gullahorn, J. T., & Gullahorn, J. E. (1963). An extension of the U-curve hypothesis. *Journal of Social Issues, 19,* 33–47.

Hackman, J. R. (1991). *Groups that work (and those that don't).* San Francisco: Jossey-Bass.

Hall, E. T. (1966). *The hidden dimension.* Garden City, NY: Doubleday.

Heine, S. J., & Lehman, D. R. (1995). Cultural variation in unrealistic optimism: Does the West feel more invulnerable than the East? *Journal of Personality and Social Psychology*, 68, 595–607.

Hofstede, G. (1980) *Culture's consequences: International differences in work related values*. Beverly Hills, CA: Sage.

House, R. J., Wright, N. S., & Aditya, R. N. (1997). Cross-cultural research on organizational leadership: A critical analysis and a proposed theory. In P. C. Earley & M. Erez (Eds.), *New perspectives on international industrial/organizational psychology* (pp. 535–625). San Francisco: New Lexington Press.

Inkson, K., Arthur, M. B., Pringle, J., & Barry, S. (1997). Expatriate assignment versus overseas experience: Contrasting models of international human resource development. *Journal of World Business*, 32 (4): 351–368.

Irving, D., & Inkson, K. (1998). *It must be Watties*. Auckland: David Bateman.

Janis, I. L. (1982). *Groupthink*. Boston: Houghton Mifflin.

Lane, H. W., DiStefano, J. J., & Maznevski, M. L. (2000). *International management behavior: Text, readings and cases*. Malden, MA: Blackwell.

Langer, E. J. (1989). *Mindfulness*. Cambridge, MA: Perseus Books.

Locke, E. A., & Latham, G. P. (1984). *Goal setting: A motivational technique that works*. Englewood, Cliffs, NJ: Prentice-Hall.

Lord, R. G., & Kernan, M. C. (1987). Scripts as determinants of purposeful behavior in organizations. *Academy of Management Review*, 12, 265–277.

Lysgaard, S. (1955). Adjustment in a foreign society: Norwegian Fulbright grantees visiting the United States. *International Social Science Bulletin*, 7, 45–51.

March, J. G. (1978). Bounded rationality, ambiguity, and the engineering of choice. *Bell Journal of Economics*, 9 (2), 587–608.

March, J., & Simon, H. (1958). *Organizations*. New York: John Wiley & Sons.

McLuhan, M. (1964). *Understanding media: The extensions of man*. New York: McGraw-Hill.

Mendenhall, M., Lane, H., Maznevski, M., & McNett, J. (Eds.). (2003). *Handbook of cross-cultural management*. Oxford: Blackwell.

Miyamoto, Y., & Ktayama, S. (2002). Cultural variation in correspondence bias: The critical role of attitude diagnosticity and socially constrained behaviour. *Journal of Personality and Social Psychology*, 83 (5), 1239–1248.

Mullen, B., & Baumeister R. F. (1987). Groups effects on self-attention and performance: Social loafing, social facilitation, and social impairment. In C. Hendrick (Ed.), *Review of personality and social psychology* (pp. 189–206). Newbury Park, CA: Sage.

Nakane, C. (1970). *Japanese society*. Berkeley: University of California Press.

Napier, N. K., & Thomas, D. C. (2004). *Managing relationships in transition economies*. New York: Praeger.

Nemeth, C. J. (1992). Minority dissent as a stimulant to group performance. In S. Worchel, W. Wood, & J. A. Simpson (Eds.), *Group process and productivity* (pp. 95–111). Newbury Park, CA: Sage.

Nisbett, R. E., & Ross, L. (1980). *Human inference*. Englewood Cliffs, NJ: Prentice-Hall.

Parker, B. (1998). *Globalization: Managing across boundaries*. London: Sage.

Pearce, J. A., & Ravlin, E. C. (1987). The design and activation of self regulating work groups. *Human Relations*, 11, 751–782.

Pelto, P. J. (1968). The difference between tight and loose societies. *Transaction*, April, 37–40.

Puffer, S. M. (1994). A portrait of Russian business leaders. *Academy of Management Executive*, 8 (1), 41–54.

Ralston, D. A., Holt, D. H., Terpstra, R. H., & Yu, K. (1997). The impact of national culture and economic ideology on managerial work values: A study of the United States, Russia, Japan, and China. *Journal of International Business Studies*, 28 (1), 177–207.

Ringelman, M. (1913). Recherches sur les moteurs animes: travails de l'homme. *Annales de l'Institut Nationale Agronomique*, 12, 1–40.

Roberts, K. H., & Boyacigiller, N. A. (1984). Cross national organizational research: The grasp of the blind men. In B. M. Staw & L. L. Cummings (Eds.), *Research in Organizational Behavior* (Vol. 6, pp. 423–475). Greenwich, CT: JAI Press.

Sagiv, L., & Schwartz, S. H. (1995). Value priorities and readiness for outgroup social contact. *Journal of Personality and Social Psychology, 69*, 437–448.

Sagiv, L., & Schwartz, S. H. (2000). A new look at national culture: Illustrative applications to role stress and managerial behavior. In N. N. Ashkanasy, C. Wilderom, and M. F. Peterson (Eds.), *The handbook of organizational culture and climate.* Newbury Park, CA: Sage.

Schein, E. H. (1985). *Organizational culture and leadership.* San Francisco: Jossey-Bass.

Schwartz, S. H. (1992). Universals in the content and structure of values: Theoretical advances and empirical tests in 20 countries. In M. P. Zanna (Ed.), *Advances in experimental social psychology* (pp. 1–65). San Diego: Academic Press.

———. (1994). Beyond individualism/collectivism: New dimensions of values. In U. Kim, H. C. Triandis, C. Kagitçibasi, S. C. Choi, and G. Yoon (Eds.), *Individualism and collectivism: Theory, applications, and methods* (pp. 85–119). Newbury Park, CA: Sage.

Schwartz, S. H., & Bilsky, W. (1990). Toward a universal psychological structure of human values. *Journal of Personality and Social Psychology, 53*, 550–562.

Shackleton, V., & Newell, S. (1994). European management selection methods: A comparison of five countries. *International Journal of Selection and Assessment, 2*, 91–102.

Shekshnia, S. V., & Puffer, S. M. (2003). Rus Wane equipment: Joint Venture in Russia. In D. C. Thomas (Ed.), *Readings and cases in international management: A cross-cultural perspective.* Thousand Oaks: CA: Sage Publications.

Smith, P. B., & Bond, M. H. (1999). *Social psychology across cultures.* Boston: Allyn and Bacon.

Sorge, A. (1993). Management in France. In D. Hickson (Ed.), *Management in Western Europe: Society, culture and organization in twelve nations* (pp. 65–87). New York: Walter de Gruyter.

Stahl, G. H., & Mendenhall, M. E. (2003). Andreas Weber's reward for success in an expatriate assignment—A return to an uncertain future. In D. C. Thomas (Ed.), *Readings and cases in international management: A cross-cultural perspective* (pp. 371–374). Thousand Oaks, CA: Sage.

The New Webster Encyclopedic Dictionary of the English Language. (1971). Chicago, IL: Consolidated Book Publishers.

Thich, Nhat Hahn (1991). *Peace is every step: The path of mindfulness in everyday life.* New York: Bantam Books.

———. (1999). *The miracle of mindfulness.* Boston, MA: Beacon Press.

Thomas, D. C. (1998). The expatriate experience: A critical review and synthesis. *Advances in International Comparative Management,* 12, 237–273.

———. (2002). *Essentials of international management: A cross-cultural perspective.* Thousand Oaks, CA: Sage.

———. (Ed.), (2003). *Readings and cases in international management: A cross-cultural perspective.* Thousand Oaks, CA: Sage.

Thomas, D. C., & Ravlin, E. C. (1995). Responses of employees to cultural adaptation by a foreign manager. *Journal of Applied Psychology,* 80, 133–146.

Thomas, D. C., Au, K., & Ravlin, E. C. (2003). Cultural variation and the psychological contract. *Journal of Organizational Behavior,* 24, 451–471.

Thomas, D. C., Ravlin, E. C., & Wallace, A.W. (1996). Effect of cultural diversity in work groups. *Research in the Sociology of Organizations,* 14, 1–33.

Triandis, H. C. (1972). *The analysis of subjective culture.* New York: John Wiley & Sons.

———. (1995). *Individualism and collectivism.* Boulder, CO: Westview.

Trompenaars, F. (1993). *Riding the waves of culture.* Burr Ridge, IL: Irwin.

Tuckman, B. W. (1965). Developmental sequence in small groups. *Psychological Bulletin,* 63 (6), 384–399.

Tversky, A., & Kahneman, D. (1974). Judgement under uncertainty: Heuristics and biases. *Science,* 85, 1124–1131.

Vance, C. M. (2002). Analysis of self-initiating career path strategies: Similarities and differences across genders. Paper presented to the annual meeting of the Academy of Management, Seattle, WA.

Walker, R. (1999). Picnic in Samoa. In N. Monin, J. Monin, & R. Walker (Eds.), *Narratives of business and society: Differing New Zealand voices* (pp. 143–153). Auckland: Longman.

Yukl, G. (1994). *Leadership in organizations,* 3rd Edition. Upper Saddle River, NJ: Prentice-Hall.

Index

acculturation, 25
adaptability, cultural, 58
adaptive behavior, 67, 69, 78, 132
adaptive skills, 120
adjustment: to overseas experience, 165, 167–170, 181; U-curve of, 167
affective autonomy, 36
African culture, as an example of cultural context, 26
American culture: as contrasted to Chinese, 30; intrusion of, 28
Americans: cross-cultural interactions involving, 100; example of cultural unawareness by, 10; favorite development activities of, 71; group behavior of, 146; intrusion of, 28; nonverbal behavior of, 114; over-optimism of, 90; stereotypic behavior of, 49; workplace scripts of, 42. *See also* United States
Anglo-Saxon peoples, as example of subcategory of European, 49
Arab countries, leadership in, 127
Asian countries: implicit communication in, 110; need for affiliation in, 90; smiling behavior in, 113, 115; use of silence in, 146
attribution, 52; definition of, 50; errors in, 50, 53, 59
Australasia, as an example of low power distance cultures, 90
automatic pilot, as a metaphor for mindlessness, 51. *See also* mindfulness; cruise control, cultural
availability heuristic, 87. *See also* heuristics

behavioral cues, 57
Brazil, as an example of collectivist behavior, 90
bribery, 94

215

86, 92, 98; strategies, 86–
87
decision: models, 83–84;
techniques, 84

egalitarianism, 35
embeddedness, 35
emotional intelligence, 16, 62
empathy, 52, 183
English language, 12, 18, 30,
71, 106, 108, 122; as a second
language, 108–109
English people: behavior by, 145;
expressions by, 46
ethics in decision making, 93,
97, 184
etiquette skills, 57
Europe, cultural differences of
selection practices in, 93
Europeans: as a broad social
category, 49; as distinct from
Japanese, 48
expatriates, 14, 73–74, 165–
167, 170–171, 175, 177–
178. See also overseas
experience
experiential learning, 62, 68, 73,
79
experiential training, 72

femininity, 34
France: leadership in, 129; social
behavior in, 56–57, 114

Gandhi, Mohandas, 125, 137
gender, as an indicator of group
membership, 48
Germany, bureaucratic negotiation in, 118
globalization, 6–8, 17, 98, 149,
182
global village, 5
groupthink, 150–152

guanxi, 92
Guatemala, cultural profile of,
38

hardiness, 21, 65–66, 74, 79
harmony, 35
heuristics, 87
hierarchy, 36
Hitler, Adolf, 125
Hofstede, Geert, 22, 31, 34, 36–
37, 39
Homer, 15
Hong Kong, and the idea of cultural convergence, 28
human nature, 22–23
human rights, fundamental, 98–
99. See also ethics in decision
making
humility, 65

Iacocca, Lee, 125
implicit communication, 109–
110
India, nonverbal behavior in,
113
individualism, 30–31; as a characteristic of the United States,
38; as a characteristic of Westerners, 143; as an important
cultural dimension, 39; as
influential in teams, 151; as
the basis for cultural generalizations, 139; as useful and
powerful, 36; in communication conventions, 109; relationship to GNP, 37. See also
collectivism
individualist(ic) cultures: characteristics of, 30; decision making in, 88, 90–91, 93; direct
communication convention in,
111; group members in, 144;
groupthink in, 151; leadership

with non-native English speakers, 108; in decision making, 97; in multicultural teams, 144, 161; in negotiation, 184

mindlessness: as cultural cruise control, 51; avoiding in cross-cultural interactions, 78; benefits of, 45; example of, 43–44; in communication, 106. *See also* cruise control, cultural

moral breach, 53

moral rules, 97

multinational corporations (MNC), 7

Muslims, cultural adaptation by, 145

negotiating styles, 117, 119

negotiation skills, 57

New Zealand, as culturally similar to Canada, 36; Maori greeting in, 114

nonverbal communication, 112–113, 184; body position, 113; distance, 113; eye contact, 116; facial expression, 115; gestures, 115; touching, 113

norms, 37; Chinese cultural, 30; cultural, 42, 58, 66–67, 95, 97, 145, 152; in communication, 102, 109, 111; in teams, 144; of employing children, 98; of hierarchy, 88; organizational, 138–139

openness, 21, 65–66, 74, 79

organization cultures, 23, 164

out-groups, 37, 39, 48, 50. *See also* in-groups

overseas assignments, 74–75, 179, 185

overseas experience, 71–74, 174, 176

personality, 22–24

philosopher's stone, 125; of leadership, 125, 127

power distance, 28, 34, 64, 90, 143–144

prejudice, 11

Proteus, 15

race: as a basis for categorization, 49; as an indicator of group membership, 48

racism, 49

relative cultural distance, 155

repatriation, 177–178, 181

rituals, 76

role modeling, 24

role models, 46, 139

Russia, leadership in, 129–131

Russians: leaders, 129–130; leadership expectations by, 131; negotiating behavior by, 119; selection decisions by, 92

Samoa, social norms in, 114

Samoans, respect for authority by, 9

satisficing, in decision making, 87

Scandinavian peoples, as a subcategory of European, 49

Schwartz, Shalom, 34, 36, 39

Schwarzenegger, Arnold, 139–140

Scots, example of cultural norms of, 41

scripts, 42–43; cultural, 45–46, 51, 85, 152, 161; in decision making, 83, 89

selective perception, 47, 52, 59

self-management, in teams, 157

About the Authors

David C. (Dave) Thomas grew up in the mountains of North Carolina, followed a respectable career, and became a vice president at Bank of America. He found it a little dull.

Kerr Inkson grew up in the Highlands of Scotland, did some degrees in psychology, and became a lecturer at Aston University in England. He found it a little dull.

Dave's life changed when he went to do an MBA. He discovered a new intellectual world, full of exciting ideas and intellectual challenges. He left the bank, and completed a PhD. He found himself especially interested in the issue of internationalism and cross-cultural differences in business. He started to publish research papers and acquired a major international reputation in the field of international management.

Kerr's life changed when he saw a job ad for an assistant professorship in management in some beautiful islands called New Zealand. In this remote corner of the globe, Kerr and his wife, Nan, found themselves living in Auckland, the city with the largest Polynesian population anywhere in the world. He was first author of a book called *Theory K,* a kind of New

Zealand version of *In Search of Excellence,* which became a local best-seller. He did a lot more writing, much of it about new forms of career—including international careers—and became a full professor.

Dave's and Kerr's lives changed again when they met one afternoon in Washington, D.C., and Kerr persuaded Dave to come and work with him at the University of Auckland. Dave and his wife, Tilley, spent several happy years in New Zealand's unique multicultural environment and traveling around Asia. Then Dave got itchy feet again and moved to Simon Fraser University in Vancouver, another multicultural city. Soon Dave too was a full professor.

In 2002 Dave published an academic book called *Essentials of International Management: A Cross-Cultural Perspective.* He thought the ideas in it were too good to be left only to academics. But he needed some help with pitching the ideas to a different audience—managers and travelers rather than students and professors. Remembering *Theory K,* he called up his good friend Kerr, now at Massey University but still in Auckland. And together Dave and Kerr wrote this book by e-mail, and, for a few weeks in the summers, together in Vancouver.

Dave and Kerr are proud of their records as teachers and researchers and members of the international business-school fraternity. They are proud of their many top academic publications and honors. But they are also proud of their desire and ability to communicate with real managers facing real challenges in the international management arena. They have both found writing *Cultural Intelligence* a hugely enjoyable experience and hope that it will bring as much enlightenment, development, and pleasure to its readers as it has to each of them.

Berrett-Koehler Publishers

Berrett-Koehler is an independent publisher of books and other publications at the leading edge of new thinking and innovative practice on work, business, management, leadership, stewardship, career development, human resources, entrepreneurship, and global sustainability.

Since the company's founding in 1992, we have been committed to creating a world that works for all by publishing books that help us to integrate our values with our work and work lives, and to create more humane and effective organizations.

We have chosen to focus on the areas of work, business, and organizations, because these are central elements in many people's lives today. Furthermore, the work world is going through tumultuous changes, from the decline of job security to the rise of new structures for organizing people and work. We believe that change is needed at all levels—individual, organizational, community, and global—and our publications address each of these levels.

To find out about our new books,
special offers,
free excerpts,
and much more,
subscribe to our free monthly eNewsletter at

www.bkconnection.com

Please see next pages for other books
from Berrett-Koehler Publishers

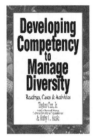